WILLIAMS-SONOMA

Casual
Outdoor Dining

GENERAL EDITOR
Chuck Williams

RECIPES
Georgeanne Brennan

PHOTOGRAPHY
Richard Eskite

Oxmoor
House®

Oxmoor
House.

OXMOOR HOUSE INC.

Oxmoor House books are distributed by
Sunset Books
80 Willow Road, Menlo Park, CA 94025
Phone: (650) 321-3600   Fax: (650) 324-1532

Vice President/General Manager: Rich Smeby
Director of Special Sales: Gary Wright
Oxmoor House and Sunset Books are divisions of
Southern Progress Corporation

WILLIAMS-SONOMA

Founder and Vice-Chairman: Chuck Williams
Book Buyer: Cecilia Michaelis

WELDON OWEN INC.

Cheif Executive Officer: John Owen
President: Terry Newell
Chief Operating Officer: Larry Partington
Vice President, International Sales: Stuart Laurence

Associate Publisher: Lisa Atwood
Project Coordinator: Judith Dunham
Consulting Editor: Norman Kolpas
Copy Editor: Sharon Silva
Design: Kari Perin, Perin+Perin
Production Director: Stephanie Sherman
Production Manager: Jen Dalton
Production Editor: Sarah Lemas
Vice President International Sales: Stuart Laurence
Co-editions Director: Derek Barton
Food Stylists: George Dolese, Susan Massey
Prop Stylist: Sara Slavin
Photo Production Coordinator: Juliann Harvey
Photo Assistants: Lara Hata, Jonathan Miller
Food Styling Assistant: Jill Sorensen
Glossary Illustrations: Alice Harth

The Williams-Sonoma Lifestyle Series
conceived and produced by Weldon Owen Inc.
814 Montgomery Street, San Francisco, CA 94133

In collaboration with Williams-Sonoma
3250 Van Ness Avenue, San Francisco, CA 94109

Separations by Colourscan Overseas Co. Pte. Ltd.
Printed in Singapore by Tien Wah Press (Pte.) Ltd.

A WELDON OWEN PRODUCTION

Copyright © 1998 Weldon Owen Inc.
All rights reserved, including the right of
reproduction in whole or in part in any form.

Library of Congress
Cataloging-in-Publication Data

First printed in 1998
10 9 8 7 6 5 4 3 2

Brennan, Georgeanne, 1943
    Casual Outdoor Dining /   by Georgeanne
Brennan ; photography by Richard Eskite.
    p. cm. — (Williams-Sonoma lifestyles)
    Includes index.
    ISBN 0-8487-2635-9
    1. Outdoor cookery.   I. Title.   II. Series.
TX823.B69 1998
    641.5'78--DC21   97-25662
                                                  CIP

A NOTE ON WEIGHTS AND MEASURES

All recipes include customary U.S. and metric
measurements. Metric conversions are based on a
standard developed for these books and have been
rounded off. Actual weights may vary.

A NOTE ON NUTRITIONAL ANALYSIS

Each recipe is analyzed for significant nutrients per
serving. Not included in the analysis are ingredients
that are optional or added to taste, or are suggested
as an alternative or substitution either in the recipe
or in the recipe introduction or accompanying tip. In
recipes that yield a range of servings, the analysis is
for the middle of that range.

Contents

Welcome

I've lost count of how many times I've heard people say that food tastes better when you eat it outdoors. Fresh air is one of the best seasonings I know.

Whether you live in the country, suburbs, or city, in a studio apartment or a twelve-room mansion, this book will help you make casual outdoor dining a part of your everyday living. On the next several pages, you'll find many easy ideas for creating a special outdoor environment, serving food, and planning menus.

The rest of the book features 49 recipes built on ingredients that are in season during the warm months of late spring, summer, and early autumn. Many of these dishes are prepared in the kitchen. Others are ideal for barbecuing. All will infuse your meals with the spirit of the great outdoors—even if you end up serving them inside!

After all, when you eat outdoors, every meal feels like a celebration.

Chuck Williams

Setting the Scene

Nature sets the scene for outdoor dining with surrounding greenery and flowers. Top: A wide-armed Adirondack chair provides not only seating but a side table for holding food or drink. Bottom: Standing atop a stack of plates for buffet-style service, a glass bowl shows off the shapes and colors of Garden Beans in Tomato-Tarragon Vinaigrette (page 49).

Choosing a Dining Spot

You don't need a garden to enjoy dining outdoors. Any place that gives you a taste of the air, a view of the sky, and pretty surroundings will do, from a backyard patio or porch to a terrace or balcony.

If you do have a garden, your options are increased, of course. Look at yours for spots that might be pleasant for dining. Maybe there's a gazebo, an arbor, or other outdoor shelter. A tree's overhanging branches might offer protection. Or a sunny patch of lawn next to a flower bed can provide the perfect terrain for setting an outdoor table or a picnic blanket.

You don't even have to go outside. Some homes have sun porches, sunny rooms, or atriums that bring the outdoors in. If yours does not, or should the weather threaten, there's no reason to abandon your plans. Just throw open a window, move the table nearby, gather up some potted plants, and create your own garden dining room.

Picking Tables and Chairs

Once you've chosen the spot, it's time to turn your attention to tables and chairs. Weather-proof patio furniture is ideal and usually can be easily moved to the selected site. A folding card table and chairs, or more attractive café or bistro furniture, work just as well. Whatever you use, keep comfort in mind. Hard-seated chairs or garden benches become more welcoming with cushions.

If space allows, or if the mood strikes, consider serving buffet style from an outdoor table or from a windowsill or garden étagère. For an inviting presentation, decorate the buffet with flowers from the garden or flowering plants in pots, or line the table surface with leaves or petals before setting down trays and serving dishes.

Providing Shade or Light

During the day, you'll probably want to have shade. Careful placement of the table or picnic blanket may be all you need to take advantage of existing shade. If not, you'll need one or more large umbrellas or, for a larger gathering, a canopy. For guests who prefer to sit in the sun, have on hand a selection of broad-brimmed hats and sunglasses, along with ample sunscreen.

If you plan to start or continue your meal after sundown, think about lighting for both the table and its surroundings. Your home may already have outdoor lights that you can turn on to enhance the garden's prettiest features. If not, many simple, inexpensive options exist. Beautiful, small lanterns or hurricane lamps can be hung from trees, ropes, or individual stakes pushed into the ground. If an electrical outlet is nearby, strings of outdoor lights, sold in a delightful range of shapes, sizes, and intensities, can be used. Try suspending them from the eaves or lacing tiny bulbs around the stays of outdoor umbrellas.

Candles look incomparably beautiful for lighting dining tables, and the more the merrier. Because breezes can quickly snuff them, it's a good idea to shelter candles in tabletop hurricane lamps or to use small votives in glass holders.

Keeping Bugs Away
Light, of course, attracts bugs. The most common way to drive them off is with citronella, a sharp, citrusy oil extracted from the Asian grass of the same name. It goes into bug-repellent candles and is sold for use in torches or lanterns.

If you are among those who dislike citronella's strong smell, there are other options. In the south of France, people prefer oil made from a kind of juniper shrub called cade, which is burned like incense. You may find it in some specialty stores. Middle Eastern and Asian insect-repellent incense coils, another possibility, are also stocked in specialty markets.

If stinging insects threaten, look for an old-fashioned wasp catcher. This glass globe, placed near a dining area, has a small receptacle that is filled with sugar water. The insects are drawn to the sweet liquid through an opening in the bottom, from which they can't escape.

More homespun still are plants whose scents people find pleasant but bugs can't stand. Bouquets of lavender, marigolds, rosemary, eucalyptus, or bay will keep pests away.

Adornments, both decorative and practical, can grace an outdoor scene. Above: Tied to a rope strung with vines, small galvanized-steel lanterns hold regular or bug-repellent citronella candles. Below: Sometimes called a fly walk, a mesh dome made of wire, rattan, or plastic keeps insects away from platters or trays of food.

Setting the Table

On a city terrace, a crisp, white table-cloth and white dishes, with gleaming sil-ver and glassware, set a spare, elegant tone. Green napkins weighted with pears echo the leaves of nearby trees.

Matching the Occasion

The table you set for a casual outdoor meal can be as elegant or relaxed as you like. It is up to you to decide what style goes best with the occasion and the menu you have chosen.

It's only natural to think first of disposable plates and cutlery for outdoor dining. After all, many of us grew up using them for our barbecued burgers and hot dogs, and we know they make cleanup easy and elimi-nate worry over breakage. Look in party-supply and specialty-kitchen stores to discover just

how well designed, sturdy, and attractive such disposable prod-ucts are today.

There are many other pretty and durable outdoor options, ranging from a new generation of plastic picnicware in beauti-ful colors and stylish designs to old-fashioned enameled tinware.

Such rough-and-tumble stuff isn't always necessary. Remem-ber that most places where you will set up your outdoor table are no farther from the kitchen than your indoor dining room is. When the occasion calls for it, don't hesitate to set the table with your best china, silver, and crystal.

Tablecloths offer you the same range of choices. Fine linens have their place on an elegant outdoor table (although it's a good idea to spread a more workaday cloth underneath to protect heirlooms from rough or stained tabletops). If you want a homey or rustic look, leave the table uncovered, espe-cially if it has a nice surface, or drape it with an old bedspread, blanket, or quilt; a traditional red- or blue-gingham cloth; or a colorful oilcloth. Choose

Three simple ways to embellish an outdoor table (left to right): a pear marking a guest's place with a card and ribbon, a handful of flowers, casually arrayed, and a container of lemons and limes decoratively scored with a citrus stripper.

complementary large napkins or, in their place, attractive small dish towels to go with any of these options.

Because anything beyond a light breeze can make most tablecloths billow, give some thought to anchoring your linens. Kitchen-supply and garden stores carry pretty weights that clip onto the cloth's corners or brackets that attach them to the table itself. Easier still, just knot each corner of the cloth around a napkin ring.

Decorating the Table

Simple decorative touches inspired by nature can subtly add to the pleasure of outdoor dining. Flowers or herbs picked from the garden or an unfussy and inexpensive bouquet from your local florist will look lovely. Just be sure to stay away from strong-smelling blooms like jasmine, gardenias, or magnolias

that might interfere with the taste buds or draw insects.

Don't display the flowers too elaborately or they may compete with the natural beauty of the setting. Slip them into an old crockery mixing bowl or pitcher, a galvanized watering can, or one or more decorative wine, vinegar, oil, or milk bottles. Or, at each place setting, put a single blossom in a small drinking glass, colored-glass water bottle, or china teacup.

Fresh seasonal produce can be used instead of cut flowers. Consider a bowl of lustrous purple eggplants, vibrant citrus fruits, purple-and-green artichokes, or bright red cherries. A fruit centerpiece can even be eaten at the end of the meal.

Cooking and Serving Food Outdoors

Taking a Natural Approach

You don't have to cook food outdoors to enjoy eating it outdoors. But even when you prepare a meal entirely in the kitchen, there are many simple things you can do to give your menu an alfresco touch.

First of all, pay attention to the seasons for the freshest, best-tasting ingredients. Sun-ripened tomatoes, for example, capture the essence of summer, while the first fresh strawberries give an outdoor menu the essence of spring.

At the same time, think about how you might be able to use produce in other ways that can add flair. The photographs on the opposite page offer a few ideas drawn from recipes in this book. The possibilities are endless. Try making edible bowls from hollowed-out cabbages or attractively cut melon halves, or use frilly kale leaves to line serving platters or individual plates.

Grilling Outdoors

The urge to grill an outdoor meal is often too hard to resist, but a few things must be kept in mind before you light the coals. Be sure not to seat guests too close to the grill or downwind from it.

Also check that your grill is in good condition and that you have enough fuel and the necessary tools and accessories. Long-handled utensils that let you reach in the grill to turn and move food without getting too close to the heat are a good idea to keep you cool and fresh. A grill basket that holds small or delicate items is another convenient tool (see glossary, page 108).

Finally, allow enough time for the fire to get going. Plan on 20–30 minutes for the coals to develop the even coat of gray ash that indicates they're ready.

Safeguarding Food Temperatures

Serving a meal in the open air can bring with it the challenge of keeping everything at the proper serving temperature. This is important not just for the sake of aesthetics, but also to prevent contamination that can lead to food poisoning.

The easiest way to make sure that hot foods stay hot and cold foods cold is to think through your menu carefully and plan the serving order with the temperatures in mind. Keep the menu simple, and don't feel that it's necessary to bring all the dishes outdoors at the same time.

If you want to serve buffet style or keep foods outdoors longer, there are easy ways to help maintain them at the right temperature. For cold dishes, place serving dishes, bowls, platters, or trays atop larger ones filled with crushed ice. Ice buckets, whether designed for that purpose or improvised from such outdoor accessories as watering cans, wagons, or wheelbarrows, will keep drinks cold. Or freeze individual bottles in a block of ice (right). During daylight, it's also a good idea to provide shade for cold foods, just as you do for your guests.

To keep hot dishes hot on outdoor warming trays, use heavy-gauge aluminum or stainless-steel units, heated by votive candles or liquid paraffin.

Many of the dishes in this book are made to be enjoyed at cool room temperature. Just be sure to take basic precautions and not leave them out for too long.

Nature lends a creative hand in outdoor cooking. Top: A trout is wrapped in grape leaves (see page 63) that shield it from the grill's heat and scent its flesh while keeping it moist. Bottom: Small rosemary branches become skewers for grilled morel mushrooms, flavoring them while they cook (see page 80).

Simple innovations keep outdoor meals cool. Top: Cherry tomatoes become edible containers for goat cheese (see page 22). Bottom: Embedded in ice, a bottle keeps drinking water cold. Place an empty bottle in a cardboard milk carton, fill the carton with water and flowers, and freeze, then remove the carton and pour drinking water into the bottle.

Beverages

Trays lined with fine linen or homespun cotton make a practical and attractive way to serve beverages outdoors. Pitchers of lemonade and iced tea, along with glassware, containers of ice cubes, and bowls of garnishes, can be set on the outdoor table for guests to help themselves.

Lemon Verbena Iced Tea

An easy-to-grow perennial herb, lemon verbena is used both fresh and dried for making tea. It has an intense lemon-herbal flavor.

6 cups (48 fl oz/1.5 l) water

6 tablespoons (1 oz/30 g) Earl Grey tea leaves

¼ cup (½ oz/15 g) dried lemon verbena leaves

ice cubes

6 lemon slices for garnish

sugar or honey to taste

❋ In a teakettle or saucepan, bring the water to a boil. Place the tea leaves and the lemon verbena leaves in a 1½–2-qt (1.5–2-l) pitcher or teapot and pour the water over them. Let stand for 5 minutes. Strain the tea and discard the leaves. Let cool, then refrigerate for about 2 hours.

❋ To serve, place ice cubes into glasses and pour in the chilled tea. Garnish with lemon slices and offer sugar or honey to add to taste.

SERVES 6

Minted Lemonade

Lemonade flavored with home-made mint syrup makes a cooling, light summertime drink.

FOR THE SYRUP

2 cups (16 fl oz/500 ml) water

1 cup (8 oz/250 g) sugar

¼ cup (⅓ oz/10 g) fresh mint leaves

1 cup (8 fl oz/250 ml) strained lemon juice

6 cups (48 fl oz/1.5 l) water

crushed ice or ice cubes

8 fresh mint sprigs for garnish

❋ To make the syrup, in a saucepan over medium-high heat, combine the water and sugar. Bring to a boil, stirring to dissolve the sugar. Cook over medium-high heat, stirring, until a light syrup forms, about 5 minutes. Remove from the heat and add the mint leaves. Let stand for about 5 minutes, then discard the leaves. Let cool, then refrigerate for about 2 hours.

❋ In a pitcher, combine the chilled syrup, lemon juice, and water and stir well. To serve, spoon ice into tall glasses and pour in the lemonade. Garnish with mint sprigs.

SERVES 8

Blackberry Milk Shake

On a hot summer day, this pale purplish milk shake is a rich yet refreshing drink or dessert to enjoy outdoors. Pass a plate of freshly baked chocolate chip cookies to eat alongside.

2 ice cubes

1 cup (4 oz/125 g) blackberries

2 tablespoons sugar

4 scoops vanilla ice cream, about 1½ cups (12 fl oz/375 ml) total

½ cup (4 fl oz/125 ml) milk

❋ Place the ice cubes in a blender or food processor and process to crush. Set aside 4 of the blackberries and add the remaining berries to the blender or food processor along with the sugar. Purée until smooth. Add the ice cream and milk and process until smooth or to the desired consistency.

❋ Pour into 2 tall glasses and garnish with the reserved berries. Serve immediately.

SERVES 2

Sparkling Wine with Crème de Pêche

For a special aperitif before an alfresco lunch or dinner, flavor sparkling wine with a touch of crème de pêche, a sweet liqueur. Similar sweet liqueurs flavored with pear, raspberry, or currant can be substituted.

1 tablespoon crème de pêche

½ cup (4 fl oz/125 ml) sparkling wine

❋ Pour the crème de pêche into a champagne flute, then pour in the sparkling wine. Serve at once.

SERVES 1

Planning Menus

All of the recipes in this book have been designed to complement one another, giving you many ways to mix and match them in menus that suit you and the occasion. The 10 menus listed here are only examples of the nearly countless possibilities. The best way to plan any casual outdoor meal, however, is to start in your garden or market, selecting vegetables and fruits at peak of season. Try to choose courses with harmonious tastes and textures that don't repeat too many ingredients. And don't be overly ambitious. Even one or two courses, enjoyed at leisure outdoors, can bring you and your guests pleasure.

Summertime Feast

Melon Halves Filled with Port
PAGE 41

Grilled Leg of Lamb
PAGE 71

Marinated Baby Squash
PAGE 34

Fresh Cherry Pie
PAGE 88

Tuscan Summer Lunch

Prosciutto-Stuffed Figs
PAGE 25

Garden-Style
Eggplant Parmesan
PAGE 64

Nectarine and Gorgonzola
Bruschetta
PAGE 103

Provençal Dinner

Grilled Asparagus
with Smoked Salmon
PAGE 30

French-Style Steaks with
Rosemary-Scented Morels
PAGE 80

Mixed Grilled Fruits
with Crème Anglaise
PAGE 98

Seaside Repast

Cherry Tomatoes
Filled with Goat Cheese
PAGE 22

Poached Salmon with
Green Grape Sauce
PAGE 79

Warm Ginger Cake with
Peaches and Cream
PAGE 106

Vegetarian Celebration

Garden Gazpacho
with Garlic Toasts
PAGE 26

Ragout of Spring Vegetables
with Almond Couscous
PAGE 76

Strawberries in Red Wine
with Vanilla Bean
PAGE 93

Summer Grill

Marinated Baby Squash
PAGE 34

Smoked Pork Loin
with Red Onion Confit
PAGE 75

Raspberry Crepes
with Ice Cream
PAGE 100

Down-Home Dinner

Corn Chowder with
Red Pepper Cream
PAGE 29

Stuffed Pork Chops
PAGE 68

Creamy Polenta

Free-Form Pear Tart
PAGE 90

Light Springtime Supper

Fava Bean and Jalapeño
Wontons
PAGE 19

Pan-Seared Salmon with
Pea Shoots and Watercress
PAGE 57

Store-Bought Lemon Sorbet

Dinner in the Arbor

Artichoke Slivers
with Thyme and Marjoram
PAGE 21

Trout Wrapped in
Grape Leaves
PAGE 63

Strawberry Sabayon
PAGE 105

Sunny Sunday Lunch

Melon Halves Filled with Port
PAGE 41

Thai Chicken Salad
PAGE 58

Filo Ice-Cream Cups
with Summer Fruit
PAGE 87

Fava Bean and Jalapeño Wontons

PREP TIME: 30 MINUTES

COOKING TIME: 20 MINUTES

INGREDIENTS

4 lb (2 kg) young, tender fava (broad)
   beans, shelled

1 teaspoon salt

1 tablespoon heavy (double) cream

1 tablespoon chopped fresh mint

1 teaspoon ground pepper

1 package (8 oz/250 g) wonton
   wrappers

4 jalapeño chiles, seeded and thinly
   sliced

canola, sunflower, or other light oil
   for deep-frying

SERVING TIP: The wontons can be
served plain or with a spicy chutney,
such as mango or peach, for dipping.

The meaty bean flavor of favas marries well with the spicy heat
of jalapeño chiles. Other starchy vegetables such as sweet
potato, taro, or peas can be cooked and puréed in place of
the favas. You will need about 1 cup (8 oz/250 g) purée.

MAKES 24 WONTONS; SERVES 4–6

❋ Place the fava beans in a saucepan and add water to cover and the
salt. Bring to a boil and cook until very tender, about 5 minutes. (If the
beans are large and mature, they will require longer cooking.) Drain
and rinse with cold running water to halt the cooking. Using the tip
of a knife or a fingernail, slit the thin skin surrounding each bean and
slip it off. Transfer the peeled beans to a blender or food processor.
Add the cream, mint, and pepper and purée until smooth.

❋ Lay a wonton wrapper on a flat surface and place 1 tablespoon of the
purée in the center. Top with a jalapeño slice. Dip a finger in water and
run a bead of moisture around the edge of the wrapper. Fold to form a
triangle and press the edges to seal. Repeat until all the purée is used,
placing the filled wontons on a piece of waxed paper or aluminum foil.
(Leftover wonton wrappers can be wrapped well and refrigerated for
up to 2 weeks.)

❋ Pour oil into a deep-fat fryer, wok, or deep saucepan to a depth of
4 inches (10 cm). Heat to 350°F (180°C) on a deep-fat frying thermometer. When the oil is hot, add a few wontons and fry until golden brown,
2–3 minutes. Using tongs or a slotted spoon, transfer to paper towels
to drain; keep warm. Fry the remaining wontons in the same manner.

❋ Transfer the wontons to a platter and serve hot or at room temperature.

NUTRITIONAL ANALYSIS PER SERVING: Calories 334 (Kilojoules 1,403); Protein 12 g;
Carbohydrates 42 g; Total Fat 13 g; Saturated Fat 2 g; Cholesterol 8 mg; Sodium 431 mg;
Dietary Fiber 6 g

Oven-Roasted Artichoke Slivers with Thyme and Marjoram

PREP TIME: 30 MINUTES

COOKING TIME: 40 MINUTES

INGREDIENTS

4 lemons

12 medium artichokes

¼ cup (2 fl oz/60 ml) extra-virgin
   olive oil

2 tablespoons minced fresh thyme

2 tablespoons minced fresh marjoram

1 teaspoon salt

1 teaspoon ground pepper

SERVING TIP: The artichoke slivers
can be paired with garlicky mayonnaise as part of an antipasto plate
that includes roasted red bell peppers (capsicums), anchovies, and
assorted black and green olives.

Herb-strewn artichokes, seasoned with the flavors of the
Mediterranean, make a simple yet elegant first course. If the
outdoor occasion is a barbecue, the slivers can be placed in
a heavy-duty aluminum foil pan and reheated over the grill.

SERVES 4–6

✶ Preheat an oven to 350°F (180°C).

✶ Fill a large bowl three-fourths full with water. Halve 2 of the lemons and squeeze their juice into the water. Working with 1 artichoke at
a time, cut off the stem flush with the base. Break off the tough outer
leaves to reach the tender inner leaves. Trim away the tough, dark green
layer around the base. Cut off the top one-third of each artichoke. Cut
the artichokes in half lengthwise and, using the edge of a small spoon,
scoop out and discard the furry inner choke from each half. Place the
trimmed halves in the lemon water. When all the artichokes are trimmed,
remove the halves one by one and cut lengthwise into slivers ¼ inch
(6 mm) thick. Return to the water until all the artichokes are prepared.

✶ Drain the artichokes, wrap in a kitchen towel, and pat dry. In a bowl,
combine the olive oil, thyme, marjoram, salt, and pepper. Add the artichokes and turn in the oil mixture to coat well.

✶ Spread the artichoke mixture on a nonstick baking sheet. Roast,
turning occasionally, until the artichokes are lightly browned and thoroughly tender, 30–40 minutes.

✶ To serve, transfer the artichokes to a platter. Cut the remaining
2 lemons into wedges and use to garnish the platter. Serve hot or at
room temperature.

NUTRITIONAL ANALYSIS PER SERVING: Calories 261 (Kilojoules 1,096); Protein 11 g;
Carbohydrates 42 g; Total Fat 12 g; Saturated Fat 2 g; Cholesterol 0 mg; Sodium 732 mg;
Dietary Fiber 16 g

Cherry Tomatoes Filled with Goat Cheese

PREP TIME: 20 MINUTES

INGREDIENTS

24 cherry tomatoes, a mixture of
   red and yellow

¼ lb (125 g) fresh goat cheese

¼ cup (⅓ oz/10 g) minced fresh basil

½ teaspoon salt

½ teaspoon ground pepper

COOKING TIP: If cherry tomatoes
are unavailable, substitute 6 small
plum (Roma) tomatoes. Remove the
cores, then cut in half lengthwise;
scoop out the pulp with a small
spoon. Divide the halves among
4 individual plates.

For a refreshing summertime appetizer, fill bite-sized cherry
tomatoes, round or pear shaped, with a savory mixture of goat
cheese flavored with basil. Minced tarragon or chervil can be
used in place of the basil.

SERVES 4

❋ Cut the top off each cherry tomato. Using a small spoon, scoop out
the pulp to make a hollow yet sturdy shell. Drain off any juice that accu-
mulates in the shells.

❋ In a bowl, combine the cheese, basil, salt, and pepper. Mix with a
fork until well blended.

❋ Using the small spoon, fill each tomato with about 1 teaspoon of the
cheese mixture. Arrange the filled tomatoes on a platter to serve.

NUTRITIONAL ANALYSIS PER SERVING: Calories 87 (Kilojoules 365); Protein 6 g;
Carbohydrates 3 g; Total Fat 6 g; Saturated Fat 4 g; Cholesterol 13 mg; Sodium 382 mg;
Dietary Fiber 1 g

Prosciutto-Stuffed Figs

PREP TIME: 15 MINUTES

INGREDIENTS

12 soft, ripe green or black figs such as Mission, Adriatic, or Kadota

24 thin slices prosciutto, about ¼ lb (125 g) total weight

½ teaspoon ground pepper

3 cups (3 oz/90 g) arugula (rocket) or baby lettuces

COOKING TIP: For a vegetarian first course, slit the figs as described and stuff with thin slices cut from a log of creamy fresh goat cheese.

The saltiness of the prosciutto and the sweetness of the figs combine to make a rich yet light appetizer. Figs are in season from summer through early fall, the perfect time of year to serve this Mediterranean-inspired first course outdoors under the spreading branches of a favorite shade tree.

SERVES 6

❀ Using a sharp knife, make a lengthwise slit in each fig, cutting only three-fourths of the way through the fruit.

❀ Rumple first 1 slice and then a second slice of the prosciutto and tuck them sumptuously into the slit of a fig. Repeat until all the figs are stuffed. Sprinkle evenly with the pepper.

❀ Divide the greens evenly among 6 individual plates. Top each with 2 stuffed figs and serve.

NUTRITIONAL ANALYSIS PER SERVING: Calories 123 (Kilojoules 517); Protein 7 g; Carbohydrates 20 g; Total Fat 3 g; Saturated Fat 1 g; Cholesterol 15 mg; Sodium 353 mg; Dietary Fiber 3 g

Garden Gazpacho with Garlic Toasts

PREP TIME: 35 MINUTES, PLUS
1 HOUR FOR CHILLING

COOKING TIME: 30 MINUTES

INGREDIENTS

FOR THE SOUP

1½ cucumbers, peeled, seeded,
and coarsely chopped

3 large, firm, ripe tomatoes, peeled
and coarsely chopped

1 red bell pepper (capsicum), seeded
and coarsely chopped

2 teaspoons lemon juice

1 tablespoon olive oil

1 clove garlic, minced

1½ tablespoons coarsely chopped
fresh cilantro (fresh coriander)

1 teaspoon ground pepper

½ teaspoon salt

FOR THE TOASTS

12 baguette slices or 4 slices coarse
country bread

2 tablespoons olive oil

2 cloves garlic

FOR THE CONDIMENTS

½ cucumber, peeled, seeded, and
chopped

1 tomato, peeled and chopped

2 or 3 green (spring) onions, chopped

2 serrano chiles, seeded, if desired,
and thinly sliced

¼ cup (⅓ oz/10 g) chopped fresh
cilantro (fresh coriander)

Andalusia's famed cold vegetable soup is a welcome first course for a meal on a hot summer day. In place of the bread that is traditionally puréed into the soup, this version calls for the soup to be ladled over crisp garlic toasts.

SERVES 4

❀ To make the soup, combine the cucumbers, tomatoes, bell pepper, lemon juice, and olive oil in a blender or food processor. Process until just blended. Do not purée; the mixture should be slightly chunky. Transfer to a nonaluminum bowl and stir in the garlic, cilantro, pepper, and salt. Cover and chill for at least 1 hour or for up to 12 hours.

❀ Meanwhile, make the toasts: Preheat an oven to 400°F (200°C). Place the bread slices on a baking sheet and drizzle evenly with the olive oil. Toast in the oven until slightly golden on top, about 15 minutes. Turn and continue to toast until golden on the second side, 10–15 minutes longer. Remove from the oven. Rub both sides of each slice with the garlic cloves. Set aside to cool.

❀ Just before serving, place the condiments in separate small bowls.

❀ To serve, place 3 baguette slices or 1 bread slice in the bottom of each soup bowl. Stir the soup and ladle it over the bread in the bowls. Accompany with the condiments, to be added to the soup as desired.

NUTRITIONAL ANALYSIS PER SERVING: Calories 207 (Kilojoules 869); Protein 4 g; Carbohydrates 25 g; Total Fat 11 g; Saturated Fat 2 g; Cholesterol 0 mg; Sodium 408 mg; Dietary Fiber 4 g

Corn Chowder with Red Pepper Cream

PREP TIME: 20 MINUTES

COOKING TIME: 45 MINUTES

INGREDIENTS

FOR THE RED PEPPER CREAM

2 large red bell peppers (capsicums)

2 tablespoons fresh oregano leaves

2 tablespoons medium-hot pure
  ground chile such as pasilla or
  1 tablespoon cayenne pepper

1 tablespoon olive oil

½ teaspoon salt

2 tablespoons heavy (double) cream

FOR THE CHOWDER

1 tablespoon chopped salt pork or
  2 slices bacon, chopped

¼ cup (1½ oz/45 g) finely diced celery

1 small yellow onion, finely diced

2 cups (16 fl oz/500 ml) chicken
  broth

4 or 5 red new potatoes, about ¾ lb
  (375 g) total weight, diced

2 tablespoons fresh thyme leaves

1 bay leaf

½ teaspoon salt

½ teaspoon ground pepper

2 cups (16 fl oz/500 ml) milk, heated

kernels from 6 ears of corn, preferably a mixture of white and yellow

Using both yellow and white kernels makes this summertime chowder particularly attractive. The red pepper cream spices each portion without overwhelming the natural sweetness of the fresh corn. Ladle the chowder into cups for an informal garden party or into bowls for a sit-down lunch or dinner.

SERVES 6–8

✺ To make the red pepper cream, preheat a broiler (griller). Halve and seed the bell peppers and place, cut sides down, on a broiler pan. Broil (grill) about 4 inches (10 cm) from the heat source until the skins are evenly blackened and blistered. Remove from the broiler, drape the peppers loosely with aluminum foil, and let stand for 10 minutes, then peel away the skins. Coarsely chop the peppers and place in a blender. Add the oregano, ground chile or cayenne, olive oil, and salt. Purée the mixture, drizzling in the cream. Transfer to a bowl and set aside.

✺ To make the chowder, place the salt pork or bacon in a heavy saucepan over medium-low heat. Cook, stirring occasionally, until the fat is rendered and the salt pork or bacon is crisp, about 5 minutes. Using a slotted spoon, transfer the crisp bits to a plate and reserve for another use. Raise the heat to medium-high, add the celery and onion to the fat in the pan, and sauté until nearly translucent, 5–6 minutes.

✺ Raise the heat to high, pour in the chicken broth, bring to a boil, and deglaze the pan, stirring to dislodge any browned bits from the pan bottom. Add the potatoes, thyme, bay leaf, salt, and pepper and return to a boil. Then cover, reduce the heat to low, and cook until the potatoes are just tender, 10–15 minutes. Add the milk and simmer for 5 minutes. Add the corn and simmer just until the corn is tender, 3–4 minutes.

✺ To serve, ladle the soup into warmed bowls. Place a spoonful of the red pepper cream on top of each serving.

NUTRITIONAL ANALYSIS PER SERVING: Calories 264 (Kilojoules 1,109); Protein 9 g; Carbohydrates 41 g; Total Fat 9 g; Saturated Fat 3 g; Cholesterol 17 mg; Sodium 680 mg; Dietary Fiber 6 g

Grilled Asparagus with Smoked Salmon and Tarragon Mayonnaise

PREP TIME: 15 MINUTES

COOKING TIME: 10 MINUTES, PLUS PREPARING FIRE

INGREDIENTS

FOR THE TARRAGON MAYONNAISE

¾ cup (6 fl oz/180 ml) mayonnaise

¼ cup (⅓ oz/10 g) minced fresh tarragon

1 teaspoon lemon juice

1 teaspoon extra-virgin olive oil

¼ teaspoon salt

1½ lb (750 g) asparagus

½ lb (250 g) smoked salmon, thinly sliced

1 lemon, cut into wedges

COOKING TIP: In place of the smoked salmon, use an equal amount of thinly sliced prosciutto—a classic Italian partner for asparagus.

Asparagus takes readily to brief grilling, which adds a mild smoky undertone to the vegetable's nutty, sweet flavor. Combined with smoked salmon, grilled asparagus is a singular beginning to a Sunday brunch or a candlelit dinner on a patio or deck. The mayonnaise can be flavored with basil or chervil in place of the tarragon.

SERVES 4

❁ Prepare a fire in a grill.

❁ To make the tarragon mayonnaise, place the mayonnaise in a bowl. Add the tarragon, lemon juice, oil, and salt and stir to mix well. Cover and refrigerate until serving.

❁ Break off any tough stem ends from the asparagus, then trim the ragged ends with a knife. Bring a frying pan three-fourths full of water to a boil. Add the asparagus and parboil for 2 minutes. Drain, rinse with cold running water until cool, and drain again.

❁ When the coals are hot, place the asparagus directly on the grill rack or in a grill basket on the rack and grill, turning as needed, until lightly marked with grill lines and just tender, 2–3 minutes on each side.

❁ To serve, make a bed of the salmon slices on 4 individual plates, dividing the salmon evenly. Arrange the grilled asparagus on top of the salmon along with some tarragon mayonnaise, again dividing evenly. Garnish with the lemon wedges.

NUTRITIONAL ANALYSIS PER SERVING: Calories 411 (Kilojoules 1,726); Protein 16 g; Carbohydrates 10 g; Total Fat 37 g; Saturated Fat 6 g; Cholesterol 37 mg; Sodium 819 mg; Dietary Fiber 1 g

Five-Tomato Salsa

PREP TIME: 15 MINUTES

INGREDIENTS

3–4 lb (1.5–2 kg) assorted tomatoes,
preferably of 5 different colors
and sizes such as small and medium,
red and yellow pear-shaped,
cherry, and beefsteak

1 red (Spanish) or yellow onion,
minced

½ cup (⅔ oz/20 g) chopped fresh
cilantro (fresh coriander)

1 teaspoon salt

1 teaspoon ground pepper

2 tablespoons lime juice

COOKING TIP: For a spicy version of
the salsa, stir in minced jalapeño or
serrano chile to taste.

A visit to a farmers' market, perhaps combined with one to
your own garden, should provide the mix of colorful tomato
varieties that this unusual salsa demands. Prepare the salsa up to
4 hours ahead and use as a dip for chips and raw vegetables; as
a topping for tacos, enchiladas, and tostadas; or as a saladlike
condiment alongside grilled meat and fish.

SERVES 6–8

❀ If using cherry tomatoes, cut in half. Chop the other tomatoes into
small pieces.

❀ Place all the tomatoes in a nonaluminum bowl and add the onion,
cilantro, salt, and pepper. Stir to mix, being careful not to break up the
tomatoes. Add the lime juice and mix again.

❀ Serve at once, or cover and refrigerate for up to 4 hours.

NUTRITIONAL ANALYSIS PER SERVING: Calories 63 (Kilojoules 265); Protein 3 g;
Carbohydrates 14 g; Total Fat 1 g; Saturated Fat 0 g; Cholesterol 0 mg; Sodium 339 mg;
Dietary Fiber 4 g

Baby Squash in Herb and Garlic Marinade

PREP TIME: 15 MINUTES, PLUS
6 HOURS FOR MARINATING

COOKING TIME: 5 MINUTES

INGREDIENTS

4 baby green zucchini (courgettes)

4 baby gold zucchini (courgettes) or
crookneck squashes

4 baby pattypan (custard) squashes

4 baby Ronde de Nice, scallopini, or
other round summer squashes

FOR THE MARINADE

½ cup (4 fl oz/125 ml) olive oil

2 tablespoons red wine vinegar

3 cloves garlic, bruised

4 bay leaves

2 teaspoons minced fresh thyme

2 teaspoons minced fresh rosemary

½ teaspoon salt

½ teaspoon ground pepper

4–8 butter (Boston) or red lettuce
leaves

¼ cup (1½ oz/45 g) thinly sliced
red bell pepper (capsicum)

A mixture of colorful baby summer squash, imbued with the flavor and aroma of fresh herbs, makes a great first impression at an outdoor sit-down dinner. If round squashes are unavailable, use all zucchini.

SERVES 4

❀ Trim the ends of the squashes but leave whole. Place on a steamer rack over boiling water, cover the steamer, and steam until tender when pierced with the tip of a knife, 2–3 minutes. Transfer to a plate.

❀ To make the marinade, in a nonaluminum bowl, combine the olive oil, vinegar, garlic, bay leaves, thyme, rosemary, salt, and pepper; mix well. Add the squashes and turn to coat with the marinade. Cover and let stand at room temperature for 6–8 hours.

❀ To serve, garnish 4 individual plates with a lettuce leaf or two and slices of bell pepper. Using a slotted spoon, remove the squashes from the marinade and divide them evenly among the plates. Serve at room temperature.

NUTRITIONAL ANALYSIS PER SERVING: Calories 144 (Kilojoules 605); Protein 2 g; Carbohydrates 5 g; Total Fat 14 g; Saturated Fat 2 g; Cholesterol 0 mg; Sodium 138 mg; Dietary Fiber 1 g

Poblano Chiles Stuffed with Ricotta and Pine Nuts

PREP TIME: 15 MINUTES

COOKING TIME: 20 MINUTES

INGREDIENTS

4 poblano chiles

¼ cup (1¼ oz/37 g) pine nuts

12 drained, oil-packed sun-dried
    tomatoes, minced

½ lb (250 g) ricotta cheese

¼ cup (⅓ oz/10 g) chopped fresh
    oregano or marjoram

½ teaspoon salt

½ teaspoon ground pepper

I teaspoon vegetable oil

3 fresh tomatoes, peeled, seeded,
    and finely chopped

minced fresh oregano or marjoram
    (optional)

COOKING TIP: For a variation, add
2 cups (¾ lb/375 g) cooked shrimp
(prawns) or shredded cooked chicken
to the ricotta mixture.

You can roast the chiles and toast the nuts ahead of time. Once the chiles are filled, you need to cook them for only a few minutes before bringing them piping hot to a table set in the garden or on a deck or patio.

SERVES 4

✬ Preheat a broiler (griller). Place the chiles on a broiler pan and broil (grill) about 4 inches (10 cm) from the heat source, turning as necessary, until the skins are evenly blackened and blistered. Remove from the broiler, drape the chiles loosely with aluminum foil, and let stand for 10 minutes, then peel away the skins. Cut a lengthwise slit in each chile, but leave the stem intact. Remove the seeds, being careful not to pierce the flesh. If necessary, rinse the peppers to remove any remaining charred skin, then pat dry. Set aside.

✬ Place a frying pan over medium-high heat and add the pine nuts. Toast, stirring, until lightly browned, 4–5 minutes. Be careful they do not burn. Transfer to a bowl and add the sun-dried tomatoes, ricotta cheese, chopped oregano or marjoram, salt, and pepper. Mix well. Divide the cheese mixture evenly among the chiles, carefully spooning it into the chiles through the slits. Pinch the edges of the slits together to close.

✬ In a nonstick frying pan over medium heat, warm the vegetable oil. When the oil is hot, place the filled chiles in the pan and gently press down on them with the back of a wooden spoon or a spatula. Cook just until the cheese begins to soften, 1–2 minutes. Turn, gently press again, and cook until the cheese is thoroughly hot, about 1 minute longer.

✬ Transfer the chiles to a warmed platter and spoon the chopped fresh tomatoes over the tops. Sprinkle with minced oregano or marjoram, if desired. Serve immediately.

NUTRITIONAL ANALYSIS PER SERVING: Calories 264 (Kilojoules 1,109); Protein 13 g; Carbohydrates 22 g; Total Fat 17 g; Saturated Fat 6 g; Cholesterol 29 mg; Sodium 426 mg; Dietary Fiber 5 g

Shrimp and Jicama in Soy-Sesame Sauce

PREP TIME: 20 MINUTES

COOKING TIME: 5 MINUTES

INGREDIENTS

¼ cup (¾ oz/20 g) sesame seeds

1 teaspoon cornstarch (cornflour)

½ teaspoon peeled and finely grated
  fresh ginger

¼ teaspoon sea salt

¼ teaspoon dry mustard

2 tablespoons soy sauce

1 tablespoon dry sherry

1 tablespoon Asian sesame oil

½ lb (250 g) shrimp (prawns), peeled
  and deveined

½ jicama, peeled and julienned

⅓ cup (⅓ oz/10 g) chopped fresh
  cilantro (fresh coriander)

PREP TIP: A jicama must be peeled
fairly thickly with a sharp knife to
remove both its dry brown skin and
the woody layer beneath it.

Jicama, sometimes called Mexican potato, has a delicate, crunchy texture and a mild flavor not unlike the texture and flavor of water chestnuts. It readily absorbs the flavor of the soy-sesame dressing. Serve this dish as a first-course salad on a bed of mixed greens, or with toothpicks for a casually passed hors d'oeuvre.

SERVES 4

✱ In a small, dry frying pan over high heat, toast the sesame seeds, stirring often, until lightly golden, about 2 minutes. Transfer to a dish and set aside.

✱ In a bowl, stir together the cornstarch, ginger, sea salt, dry mustard, soy sauce, and sherry.

✱ In a sauté pan over medium-high heat, warm the sesame oil. Add the shrimp, reduce the heat to medium, and cook, stirring, until the shrimp are opaque, about 2 minutes. Transfer the shrimp and any pan juices to the bowl holding the soy-sherry mixture and turn to coat the shrimp. Add the jicama and turn to coat as well.

✱ Arrange the shrimp and jicama on 4 individual plates. Top with the sesame seeds and the cilantro and serve hot or warm.

NUTRITIONAL ANALYSIS PER SERVING: Calories 175 (Kilojoules 735); Protein 12 g; Carbohydrates 11 g; Total Fat 9 g; Saturated Fat 1 g; Cholesterol 71 mg; Sodium 679 mg; Dietary Fiber 5 g

Melon Halves Filled with Port

PREP TIME: 5 MINUTES

INGREDIENTS

2 ripe cantaloupes

I cup (8 fl oz/240 ml) port wine

PREP TIP: Small honeydew melons are also complemented by wine. Use a sweet white dessert wine such as Sauternes or late-harvest Riesling, whose color and taste are well suited to the pale, spicy honeydew.

When the highly perfumed Charentais and cantaloupe melons are at their prime, this is a classic summertime starter in Provençal restaurants and homes alike. If desired, garnish with sprigs of fresh mint.

SERVES 4

❀ Cut the melons in half crosswise. Scoop out and discard the seeds.

❀ Place each half on an individual plate or in a shallow bowl. If necessary, cut a thin slice from the bottom of each half so that it sits flat without tipping.

❀ Pour ¼ cup (2 fl oz/60 ml) of the port into each seed cavity. Serve immediately.

NUTRITIONAL ANALYSIS PER SERVING: Calories 185 (Kilojoules 777); Protein 2 g; Carbohydrates 29 g; Total Fat 1 g; Saturated Fat 0 g; Cholesterol 0 mg; Sodium 29 mg; Dietary Fiber 2 g

Mediterranean Salad Platter

PREP TIME: 25 MINUTES

COOKING TIME: 10 MINUTES,
    PLUS PREPARING FIRE

INGREDIENTS

4 small to medium zucchini (cour-
    gettes), thinly sliced lengthwise

3 red bell peppers (capsicums)

2 tablespoons olive oil

4 large tomatoes, sliced

2 large red (Spanish) onions, thinly
    sliced

6 oz (185 g) feta cheese, crumbled

½ cup (2½ oz/75 g) Mediterranean-
    style oil-packed black olives

½ cup (2½ oz/75 g) Kalamata olives or
    other brine-cured black olives

½ cup (2½ oz/75 g) Mediterranean-
    style green olives

2 tablespoons capers

6 anchovy fillets packed in olive oil,
    drained (optional)

FOR THE DRESSING

½ cup (4 fl oz/125 ml) extra-virgin
    olive oil

⅓ cup (3 fl oz/80 ml) balsamic vinegar

½ teaspoon salt

½ teaspoon ground pepper

Mediterranean vegetables, cheese, various olives, and anchovies come together in this easy-to-assemble outdoor party fare. When it is time to serve the salad, simply arrange the elements on a platter and drizzle with the dressing. The vegetables can be grilled a day in advance.

SERVES 6–8

❀ Prepare a fire in a grill. Brush the zucchini and bell peppers with the olive oil.

❀ When the coals are hot, place the zucchini directly on the grill rack or in a grill basket on the rack and grill until lightly golden on the first side, 4–5 minutes. Turn and cook until golden on the second side, about 3 minutes longer. At the same time, place the bell peppers directly on the grill rack and grill, turning as necessary, until the skins are evenly blackened and blistered, 4–5 minutes on each side. Remove the zucchini and set aside. Place the peppers on a plate, cover with aluminum foil, and let stand for 10 minutes, then peel away the skins. Cut the peppers in half lengthwise and remove the seeds. Cut the halves lengthwise into thin strips.

❀ To serve, arrange the zucchini, bell peppers, tomato slices, and onion slices on a platter. Top with the feta cheese, all the olives, the capers, and the anchovies, if using.

❀ To make the dressing, in a bowl, combine the olive oil, balsamic vinegar, salt, and pepper; mix well. Drizzle the dressing evenly over the salad and serve.

NUTRITIONAL ANALYSIS PER SERVING: Calories 401 (Kilojoules 1,684); Protein 8 g; Carbohydrates 24 g; Total Fat 33 g; Saturated Fat 7 g; Cholesterol 22 mg; Sodium 1,307 mg; Dietary Fiber 4 g

Double-Bread and Chicken Salad with Tomatoes and Arugula

PREP TIME: 20 MINUTES

COOKING TIME: 40 MINUTES

INGREDIENTS

FOR THE CROUTONS

2 cups (4 oz/125 g) cubed day-old
    baguette (1-inch/2.5-cm cubes)

2 tablespoons extra-virgin olive oil

2 cloves garlic

FOR THE DRESSING

⅓ cup (3 fl oz/80 ml) extra-virgin
    olive oil

3 tablespoons red wine vinegar

2 cloves garlic, crushed

½ teaspoon salt

½ teaspoon ground pepper

FOR THE SALAD

2 lb (1 kg) tomatoes, chopped

canola, sunflower, or other light oil
    for frying

1 cup (4 oz/125 g) seasoned, fine
    dried bread crumbs

1½ lb (750 g) boneless chicken
    breast, cut into 1-inch (2.5-cm)
    pieces

1 cup (2 oz/60 g) coarsely chopped
    arugula (rocket)

Summertime's sweet, juicy tomatoes are delectable when combined with garlicky croutons, crisp crumb-coated bits of chicken breast, and aromatic arugula. Although this main-course salad tastes best when the chicken is hot, it can also be served cold or warm. Basil can be used in place of the arugula.

SERVES 4–6

✺ To make the croutons, preheat an oven to 400°F (200°C). Spread the bread cubes on a baking sheet and drizzle evenly with the olive oil. Bake until lightly golden, about 15 minutes. Stir and continue to bake until golden brown, about 10 minutes longer. Let cool for a few minutes. Rub with the garlic. Set aside.

✺ Meanwhile, make the dressing: In a large bowl, combine the olive oil, vinegar, garlic, salt, and pepper; mix well.

✺ To make the salad, add the tomatoes to the bowl with the dressing and turn in the dressing until well coated. Set aside. Pour oil into a sauté pan to a depth of 1 inch (2.5 cm). Place over medium-high heat and heat until a bread cube dropped into the oil sizzles immediately upon contact. While the oil is heating, place the bread crumbs on a plate. Roll the chicken pieces, a few at a time, in the crumbs until coated. Transfer to a sheet of waxed paper. When you have coated enough pieces to fill the sauté pan in a single layer, spoon the chicken into the pan and fry until just cooked through, 3–4 minutes. Using a slotted spoon, transfer to paper towels to drain. Repeat until all the chicken is cooked.

✺ Add the hot chicken to the bowl of tomatoes and dressing. Then add the arugula, reserving 1 tablespoon for garnish, and all but 5 or 6 of the croutons. Turn all the salad ingredients to coat the croutons and the chicken with the dressing.

✺ To serve, scoop the salad into a serving bowl. Top with the reserved croutons and arugula.

NUTRITIONAL ANALYSIS PER SERVING: Calories 665 (Kilojoules 2,793); Protein 39 g; Carbohydrates 39 g; Total Fat 40 g; Saturated Fat 5 g; Cholesterol 79 mg; Sodium 1,099 mg; Dietary Fiber 4 g

Broiled Snapper on Toasted Sourdough

PREP TIME: 20 MINUTES

COOKING TIME: 8 MINUTES

INGREDIENTS

FOR THE TARTAR SAUCE

¾ cup (6 fl oz/180 ml) mayonnaise

1½ tablespoons Dijon mustard

1½ tablespoons minced yellow onion

1½ tablespoons minced sweet pickle

1½ teaspoons pickle juice

1 teaspoon lemon juice

½ teaspoon ground pepper

1 lb (500 g) red or other snapper fillet, about ½ inch (12 mm) thick

2 tablespoons unsalted butter, melted

1 teaspoon ground pepper

½ teaspoon salt

1 lemon, halved

4 sourdough rolls, split and toasted, or 8 slices sourdough bread, toasted

8 romaine (cos), butter (Boston), or red lettuce leaves

Toasted bread generously spread with a tangy sauce of mayonnaise and mustard laced with pickles and onions pairs perfectly with the broiled fish in this sandwich. The sandwiches can be prepared and served assembled, or for an easy outdoor lunch or supper, the fish can be grilled and the sauce and other components set out on a table for guests to make their own sandwiches.

MAKES 4 SANDWICHES; SERVES 4

❀ Preheat a broiler (griller).

❀ To make the tartar sauce, in a bowl, combine the mayonnaise, mustard, onion, pickle, pickle juice, lemon juice, and pepper. Stir until blended. Cover and refrigerate until needed.

❀ Cut the snapper fillet into 4 equal pieces. Brush each fillet on both sides with the melted butter. Sprinkle on both sides with the pepper and salt. Place the fillets on a broiler pan and slip under the broiler about 6 inches (15 cm) from the heat source. Broil (grill), turning once, just until the flesh flakes easily with a fork, 3–4 minutes on each side. Do not overcook.

❀ Remove from the broiler and squeeze the juice from the lemon halves evenly over the fillets. Spread the cut sides of the rolls or the 8 bread slices with some of the tartar sauce. Top the bottom halves of the rolls or 4 of the bread slices with the hot fish and lettuce leaves, dividing evenly. Top with the remaining roll halves or bread slices. Serve on individual plates.

NUTRITIONAL ANALYSIS PER SERVING: Calories 645 (Kilojoules 2,709); Protein 30 g; Carbohydrates 37 g; Total Fat 42 g; Saturated Fat 9 g; Cholesterol 82 mg; Sodium 1,122 mg; Dietary Fiber 2 g

Garden Beans in Tomato-Tarragon Vinaigrette

PREP TIME: 20 MINUTES, PLUS
3 HOURS FOR MARINATING

COOKING TIME: 40 MINUTES

INGREDIENTS

1 lb (500 g) assorted young, tender snap beans, trimmed

2 lb (1 kg) assorted shelling beans, shelled

FOR THE DRESSING

1 large, very ripe tomato, peeled, seeded, and minced

2 shallots, minced

1 clove garlic, minced

½ cup (4 fl oz/125 ml) olive oil

⅓ cup (3 fl oz/80 ml) red wine vinegar

2 tablespoons minced fresh tarragon

1 teaspoon ground pepper

½ teaspoon salt

COOKING TIP: Before cooking, sample your shelling beans for maturity. Bite into 2 or 3 beans. If your teeth meet resistance, the beans have begun to dry and they will require longer cooking than those that can be easily bitten.

In summer and early fall, shelling beans and snap beans are ready for picking. The more colors and types you can incorporate into this salad, the better. Seek out yellow wax beans, small Blue Lake beans, black-eyed peas, green snap beans, purple-podded beans, pale green lima beans, mottled cranberry beans, and any regional or heirloom varieties at local farmers' markets.

SERVES 4–6

❋ Place the snap beans on a steamer rack over gently boiling water, cover, and steam until tender but still bright colored, about 10 minutes. Remove from the steamer and rinse with cold running water to halt the cooking and to retain the color. Set aside.

❋ Working in batches, place each variety of shelling bean on the steamer rack over gently boiling water, cover, and steam until the beans are tender and have lost all hint of crunchiness. The cooking time will depend upon the size and maturity of the beans: some may cook in only 10 minutes, while others may take 30 minutes or longer. Remove from the steamer and rinse with cold running water to halt the cooking. Set aside.

❋ To make the dressing, combine the tomato, shallots, garlic, olive oil, vinegar, tarragon, pepper, and salt in a large nonaluminum bowl. Mix well. Add the snap beans and the shelling beans and turn in the dressing until well coated. Cover and refrigerate for at least 3 hours or preferably overnight.

❋ Serve chilled or at room temperature.

NUTRITIONAL ANALYSIS PER SERVING: Calories 277 (Kilojoules 1,163); Protein 6 g; Carbohydrates 17 g; Total Fat 22 g; Saturated Fat 3 g; Cholesterol 0 mg; Sodium 259 mg; Dietary Fiber 2 g

Shredded Beef with Avocado-Tomatillo Salsa

PREP TIME: 20 MINUTES

COOKING TIME: 5 HOURS

INGREDIENTS

1 tri-tip or boneless chuck roast, 2 lb (1 kg)

1 teaspoon salt

1 teaspoon ground pepper

4 ancho chiles

2 yellow onions, halved

4 cloves garlic, crushed

1 tablespoon fresh oregano leaves

FOR THE SALSA

20 tomatillos, husks removed

6 Hungarian wax chiles, seeded and minced

4 serrano chiles, seeded and minced

¼ cup (⅓ oz/10 g) chopped fresh cilantro (fresh coriander)

¼ cup (1½ oz/45 g) minced yellow onion

2 cloves garlic, minced

½ teaspoon salt

3 avocados, halved, pitted, and peeled

juice of 4 limes (about 2 tablespoons)

Beef cooked with chiles and oregano for several hours becomes pleasantly spicy and so soft it can be shredded effortlessly with a fork. Serve on warmed tortillas, and accompany with a salad of crisp romaine (cos) lettuce and a bowl of black beans.

SERVES 4–6

✳ Preheat an oven to 325°F (165°C).

✳ Rub the roast with the salt and pepper. Place in a heavy ovenproof baking dish with a tight-fitting lid. Crumble the ancho chiles over the roast and add the onion halves, garlic, and oregano. Cover and place in the oven. Roast until the meat is juicy and easily shreds with a fork, about 5 hours.

✳ Just before the beef is ready, make the salsa: Bring a saucepan three-fourths full of water to a boil. Add the tomatillos and parboil until softened, about 5 minutes. Drain and let cool. Mince the tomatillos and place in a bowl. Add the chiles, cilantro, onion, garlic, and salt. Stir to combine. Add the avocado halves and, using a fork, mash into the tomatillo mixture. The salsa should be a little chunky. Stir in the lime juice.

✳ Remove the meat from the oven and discard the onions. Using a fork, shred the beef in the dish, blending it with the juices. Keep warm until ready to serve, or refrigerate when cool and reheat over low heat to serve.

✳ Serve the beef warm with the salsa.

NUTRITIONAL ANALYSIS PER SERVING: Calories 769 (Kilojoules 3,230); Protein 42 g; Carbohydrates 33 g; Total Fat 54 g; Saturated Fat 16 g; Cholesterol 123 mg; Sodium 783 mg; Dietary Fiber 4 g

PREP TIP: To remove the sticky, papery husks from tomatillos, hold the tomatillos under warm running water. The husks will come right off.

Cilantro, Cucumber, and Red Chile Salad

PREP TIME: 10 MINUTES,
PLUS 30 MINUTES FOR
MARINATING

INGREDIENTS

2 cucumbers, peeled and thinly sliced

1 cup (1½ oz/45 g) coarsely chopped fresh cilantro (fresh coriander)

3 small dried red chiles such as árbol, pequín, or bird's-eye, seeded

½ teaspoon salt

¼ cup (2 fl oz/60 ml) unseasoned rice vinegar

2 tablespoons canola, sunflower, or other light oil

PREP TIP: If you can find English (hothouse) cucumbers, which have thin green skins without a trace of bitterness, there is no need to peel them. Their green color will add to the salad's visual appeal.

With its hints of both Southwestern and Asian flavors, this salad makes a good accompaniment to roasted or grilled meats or poultry. It can also be tossed with mixed greens and cooked shrimp (prawns) and served as a main-course salad.

SERVES 4

❋ In a nonaluminum bowl, combine the cucumbers and cilantro, then crumble in the dried chiles. Sprinkle with the salt and add the vinegar and oil. Turn to coat well.

❋ Let stand for 30 minutes to allow the flavors to blend. Serve at room temperature.

NUTRITIONAL ANALYSIS PER SERVING: Calories 83 (Kilojoules 349); Protein 1 g; Carbohydrates 5 g; Total Fat 7 g; Saturated Fat 1 g; Cholesterol 0 mg; Sodium 282 mg; Dietary Fiber 1 g

Grilled Eggplant, Red Onion, and Pepper Sandwich with Basil Mayonnaise

PREP TIME: 25 MINUTES,
PLUS 30 MINUTES FOR
MARINATING

COOKING TIME: 25 MINUTES,
PLUS PREPARING FIRE

INGREDIENTS

¼ cup (2 fl oz/60 ml) olive oil

2 tablespoons fresh thyme leaves

2 tablespoons fresh rosemary leaves

½ teaspoon ground pepper

¼ teaspoon salt

2 globe or 4 Asian (slender) eggplants (aubergines), thinly sliced

2 large red (Spanish) onions, thinly
sliced

3 large red bell peppers (capsicums)

FOR THE MAYONNAISE

2 cloves garlic

1 tablespoon olive oil

¼ cup (⅓ oz/10 g) minced fresh basil

½ teaspoon chopped fresh thyme

¾ cup (6 fl oz/180 ml) mayonnaise

2 baguettes, each split lengthwise
and then cut crosswise into thirds

6–12 red lettuce leaves

These sandwiches are easy to assemble, as the eggplant, red peppers, and mayonnaise can be prepared up to 2 days in advance, leaving only the layering of the ingredients to be done before serving.

SERVES 6

❋ Prepare a fire in a grill.

❋ In a large nonaluminum bowl or shallow dish, combine the olive oil, thyme, rosemary, pepper, and salt, and stir to mix. Add the sliced eggplants and onions and the whole peppers and turn to coat well. Let stand at room temperature for about 30 minutes.

❋ While the vegetables are marinating, make the mayonnaise: In a blender or food processor, combine the garlic, olive oil, basil, and thyme. Purée until smooth. Add the mayonnaise and process just until blended. Transfer to a bowl, cover, and refrigerate until needed.

❋ When the coals are medium-hot, place the eggplants, onions, and peppers directly on the grill rack or in a grill basket on the rack. Cook the eggplant slices until a golden crust forms on the first side, 7–8 minutes. Turn and cook on the second side until a golden crust forms and the interior is cooked through, 6–7 minutes longer. Cook the onions until lightly browned on the first side, 4–5 minutes. Turn and cook until lightly browned on the second side, 3–4 minutes. Cook the peppers, turning as necessary, until the skins are evenly blackened and blistered, 4–5 minutes on each side.

❋ Remove the eggplants and onions and set aside. Place the peppers on a plate, cover with aluminum foil, and let stand for 10 minutes, then peel away the skins. Cut the peppers in half lengthwise and remove the seeds. Cut the halves lengthwise in half.

❋ Spread the cut sides of the baguettes evenly with the mayonnaise. Top the bottom halves of the baguettes with the eggplants, onions, bell peppers, and lettuce leaves, dividing evenly. Top with the remaining baguette halves. Serve on individual plates.

NUTRITIONAL ANALYSIS PER SERVING: Calories 609 (Kilojoules 2,558); Protein 11 g; Carbohydrates 64 g; Total Fat 36 g; Saturated Fat 5 g; Cholesterol 16 mg; Sodium 728 mg; Dietary Fiber 7 g

Pan-Seared Salmon with Pea Shoots and Watercress

PREP TIME: 15 MINUTES

COOKING TIME: 10 MINUTES

INGREDIENTS

⅔ cup (5 fl oz/160 ml) extra-virgin olive oil

⅓ cup (3 fl oz/80 ml) lemon juice, preferably from Meyer lemons

3 shallots, minced

½ teaspoon salt

½ teaspoon ground pepper

¼ teaspoon sugar, if needed

5 cups (5 oz/155 g) watercress leaves

5 cups (5 oz/155 g) pea shoots

FOR THE SALMON
1½ teaspoons salt

8 salmon fillets, each about ⅓ lb (5 oz/155 g) and ½ inch (12 mm) thick

1 teaspoon ground pepper

½ cup (4 fl oz/125 ml) dry white wine

8 tablespoons (4 fl oz/125 ml) lemon juice, preferably from Meyer lemons

4 tablespoons (2 fl oz/60 ml) water

Once cooked, the salmon and its pan juices become a topping for a tangle of sprightly flavored greens dressed with a lemon vinaigrette. Pea shoots, the clippings from young pea plants, have a mild pealike flavor that blends well with the peppery watercress. They are sold in Asian markets, but if you can't find them, substitute baby arugula (rocket), spinach, or lettuce. Searing the salmon fillets can be accomplished as easily over a fire in a grill as on a stove top.

SERVES 8

❀ In a large bowl, combine the olive oil, lemon juice, shallots, salt, and pepper. Add the sugar if not using juice from Meyer lemons. Mix until well blended.

❀ Add the watercress leaves and pea shoots to the dressing and turn gently to coat well. Divide the greens evenly among 8 individual plates.

❀ To prepare the salmon, sprinkle the salt in a wide, heavy frying pan and place over medium-high heat until nearly smoking. Add the salmon fillets and sear for 2 minutes on one side. Turn and sear for 1 minute on the second side. Sprinkle with the pepper. Reduce the heat to low, then pour in the white wine and 2 tablespoons of the lemon juice. Cover and cook until the juices are nearly absorbed and the fish is halfway cooked, about 3 minutes. Uncover and pour in 2 more tablespoons of the lemon juice and 3 tablespoons of the water. Re-cover and cook just until the fish flakes easily with a fork, about 3 minutes longer. Most of the pan juices will have been absorbed.

❀ Place a salmon fillet on each mound of greens. Raise the heat to high, add the remaining 4 tablespoons lemon juice and the remaining 1 tablespoon water, and deglaze the pan, stirring to dislodge any browned bits from the pan bottom. Pour the pan juices evenly over the fish and serve.

NUTRITIONAL ANALYSIS PER SERVING: Calories 422 (Kilojoules 1,772); Protein 31 g; Carbohydrates 10 g; Total Fat 28 g; Saturated Fat 4 g; Cholesterol 78 mg; Sodium 628 mg; Dietary Fiber 3 g

Thai Chicken Salad

PREP TIME: 15 MINUTES

INGREDIENTS

2 chicken breast halves, ½ lb (250 g)
each

salt and ground pepper to taste

½ small head green cabbage

½ small head iceberg lettuce

½ cup (4 fl oz/125 ml) unseasoned
rice vinegar

3 tablespoons fish sauce

⅓ teaspoon Asian sesame oil

2 teaspoons sugar

2 tablespoons seeded and minced
serrano chile

1 small avocado, pitted, peeled, and
finely diced

½ cup (¾ oz/20 g) chopped fresh
cilantro (fresh coriander)

PREP TIP: To remove the pit from
an avocado half, hold the half in one
palm. Holding a sharp knife in your
other hand, carefully strike the pit
so that the blade lodges in it. Twist
the knife to remove the pit from the
avocado half.

Shredded chicken, diced avocado, and shredded greens are
dressed with the flavors of Southeast Asia to make a light main-
course salad for the outdoor table. Fish sauce, a salty seasoning,
is sold in Asian markets. For a festive presentation on the outdoor table, omit the diced avocado from the salad and spoon
the salad into 4 avocado halves.

SERVES 4

❀ Preheat an oven to 350°F (180°C).

❀ Place the chicken breast halves, skin side up, on a rack in a roasting
pan. Sprinkle with salt and pepper. Bake until the juices no longer run
pink when the chicken is pierced to the bone with a knife, 30–35 minutes. Remove from the oven and let cool. Remove and discard the skin.
Remove the chicken from the bone and cut into ½-inch (12-mm) cubes.

❀ Place the cabbage half on a cutting board and, using a large knife,
slice across the cut side into the thinnest possible shreds. Measure out
2 cups (6 oz/185 g); reserve any left over for another use. Cut and measure the lettuce in the same way. Set aside.

❀ In a bowl, stir together the vinegar, fish sauce, sesame oil, and sugar.
Add the chicken and stir to coat with the dressing. Add the cabbage, lettuce, and chile and toss to combine. Add the diced avocado and gently
turn the salad to distribute evenly.

❀ Divide the salad among 4 individual plates or bowls. Sprinkle with
the cilantro and serve.

NUTRITIONAL ANALYSIS PER SERVING: Calories 223 (Kilojoules 937); Protein 21 g;
Carbohydrates 14 g; Total Fat 10 g; Saturated Fat 2 g; Cholesterol 46 mg; Sodium 511 mg;
Dietary Fiber 3 g

Niçoise Salad with Grilled Tuna

PREP TIME: 20 MINUTES

COOKING TIME: 30 MINUTES,
    PLUS PREPARING FIRE

INGREDIENTS

- 1 lb (500 g) boiling potatoes such as White Rose, Yellow Finn, or Red Rose
- ¾ teaspoon salt
- 1 lb (500 g) young, thin green beans, trimmed
- 8 whole anchovies packed in salt or 16 anchovy fillets in olive oil
- 2 cups (2 oz/60 g) mixed young lettuces
- 5 tomatoes, thinly sliced
- 1 cucumber, peeled and thinly sliced
- 4 hard-boiled eggs, peeled and thinly sliced

FOR THE DRESSING

- ½ cup (4 fl oz/125 ml) extra-virgin olive oil
- ¼ cup (2 fl oz/60 ml) red wine vinegar
- 1 clove garlic, minced
- ½ teaspoon salt
- ½ teaspoon ground pepper

FOR THE TUNA

- 1⅓ lb (655 g) tuna fillet, about ½ inch (12 mm) thick
- ¼ teaspoon salt
- ¼ teaspoon ground pepper
- ½ cup (2½ oz/75 g) Mediterranean-style oil-packed black olives
- 1 tablespoon capers (optional)

From Nice, on the French Riviera, comes this simply composed salad rich in the flavors of the land and the sea. The salad can be served at room temperature, making it an excellent candidate for enjoying outdoors.

SERVES 6

❀ In a saucepan, combine the potatoes with water to cover by 2–3 inches (5–7.5 cm) and ½ teaspoon of the salt. Bring to a boil, reduce the heat to medium-low, and cook until tender, about 20 minutes. Drain, rinse with cold running water, and let stand until cool enough to handle, then peel and cut into ½-inch (12-mm) cubes. Set aside.

❀ Meanwhile, bring a saucepan three-fourths full of water to a boil. Add the remaining ¼ teaspoon salt and the green beans. Cook until the beans are just tender, 5–7 minutes. Drain, rinse with cold running water until cool, and drain again. Set aside.

❀ Prepare a fire in a grill.

❀ If using salted anchovies, rinse and pat dry. Cut lengthwise along the backbone of each anchovy and pull the bone free. Discard the backbone, head, and tail. If using oil-packed anchovies, drain well. Arrange the lettuces on a serving platter. Place the potatoes, green beans, tomatoes, cucumber, and eggs in separate piles on top of the lettuces. Drape the anchovy fillets on top.

❀ To make the dressing, in a small bowl, combine the olive oil, vinegar, garlic, salt, and pepper; mix well. Pour the dressing over the salad.

❀ Cut the tuna into 6 serving pieces. Rub on both sides with the salt and pepper. When the coals are hot, place the tuna directly on the grill rack. Alternatively, preheat a broiler (griller), place the tuna on a broiler pan, and slip under the broiler about 6 inches (15 cm) from the heat source. Cook, turning once, until done as desired when cut into the center with a knife, 2–3 minutes on each side for rare or about 6 minutes on each side for well done.

❀ Transfer the tuna to the platter, scatter the olives and the capers (if using) on top, and serve.

NUTRITIONAL ANALYSIS PER SERVING: Calories 530 (Kilojoules 2,226); Protein 35 g; Carbohydrates 27 g; Total Fat 33 g; Saturated Fat 6 g; Cholesterol 186 mg; Sodium 1,290 mg; Dietary Fiber 4 g

Trout Wrapped in Grape Leaves with Lemon-Basil Mayonnaise

PREP TIME: 35 MINUTES

COOKING TIME: 10 MINUTES,
    PLUS PREPARING FIRE

INGREDIENTS

FOR THE SAUCE

¼ cup (¼ oz/7 g) fresh basil leaves

1 cup (8 fl oz/250 ml) mayonnaise

¼ cup (2 fl oz/60 ml) lemon juice

1 tablespoon olive oil

½ teaspoon ground pepper

¼ teaspoon salt

4 trout, about 10 oz (315 g) each

2 lemons, halved, plus 4 slices for
    garnish (optional)

½ teaspoon salt

½ teaspoon ground pepper

8 long fresh thyme sprigs

16–24 large fresh grape leaves

4 fresh basil sprigs (optional)

SERVING TIP: Peeling away the grape leaves can be a messy job if they have burned slightly, as they will crumble. Provide two sets of plates for each diner: one on which to peel away the leaves and another on which to place the ready-to-eat fish.

Wrapping fish in fresh grape leaves for grilling protects the fish from the direct heat of the coals and permits the fish to steam while infusing its juicy, succulent flesh with a hint of the leaves' flavor. If fresh leaves are unavailable, substitute leaves packed in brine and rinse well before using.

SERVES 4

❋ Prepare a fire in a grill.

❋ To make the sauce, chop or mince the basil in a food processor or by hand. Add the mayonnaise, lemon juice, olive oil, pepper, and salt and process or stir until thoroughly mixed. Taste and adjust the seasonings. Cover and refrigerate until serving.

❋ Rub the cavities and outside skin of the trout with the lemon halves, squeezing a little juice on them as you do so. Sprinkle inside and out with the salt and pepper, then tuck 2 thyme sprigs inside each cavity. Lay 1 grape leaf on a work surface and place 1 fish on top. Wrap the leaf around the fish. Repeat with more leaves until the fish is snugly wrapped in two layers of leaves. Wrap all the fish in the same manner. Fasten the leaves with toothpicks or skewers, if necessary.

❋ When the coals are medium-hot, place the wrapped trout, seam side down, directly on the grill rack or in a grill basket directly on the grill. Grill until the grape leaves are slightly browned on the first side, about 5 minutes. Turn and cook until browned on the second side, 4–5 minutes longer. Remove some of the grape leaves from 1 trout and test the flesh with a fork; it should just flake easily.

❋ To serve, place the trout on 4 individual plates and let diners unwrap their own fish; provide a plate for the discarded grape leaves. (Alternatively, remove the grape leaves yourself and place the fish on individual plates.) Garnish each plate with a lemon slice and a basil sprig, if desired. Pass the sauce at the table.

NUTRITIONAL ANALYSIS PER SERVING: Calories 639 (Kilojoules 2,684); Protein 30 g; Carbohydrates 4 g; Total Fat 56 g; Saturated Fat 9 g; Cholesterol 113 mg; Sodium 797 mg; Dietary Fiber 0 g

Garden-Style Eggplant Parmesan

PREP TIME: 30 MINUTES

COOKING TIME: 1¾ HOURS

INGREDIENTS

FOR THE SAUCE

2 tablespoons olive oil

2 cloves garlic, chopped

3 lb (1.5 kg) fully ripe tomatoes, peeled and coarsely chopped

1 tablespoon chopped fresh marjoram or oregano

salt to taste

4 or 5 small or 2 medium-large eggplants (aubergines), cut into slices ½ inch (12 mm) thick

4 tablespoons (2 fl oz/60 ml) extra-virgin olive oil

½ teaspoon salt

8–10 fresh thyme sprigs or 2–3 tablespoons fresh thyme leaves

FOR THE FILLING

6 oz (185 g) mozzarella cheese, shredded

¼ cup (⅓ oz/10 g) chopped fresh oregano

¼ cup (1 oz/30 g) grated Parmesan cheese

1½ tablespoons unsalted butter, cut into bits

PREP TIP: If using large eggplants, select the hardest ones you can find, as they will have the fewest seeds.

Although this dish can be made throughout the summer, it is a particularly good season ender. Late-harvest tomatoes allowed to ripen to a deep, dark red make a sauce that is sublimely sweet and full of flavor.

SERVES 4–6

❋ To make the sauce, in a large saucepan over medium heat, warm the olive oil. Add the garlic and sauté until translucent, 2–3 minutes; do not allow to brown. Add the tomatoes and marjoram or oregano, raise the heat to high, and bring to a boil. Reduce the heat to medium-low and simmer, uncovered, until the tomatoes have cooked down to a sauce, 30–40 minutes. Taste and add salt if needed.

❋ Preheat an oven to 450°F (230°C).

❋ Place the eggplant slices in a single layer on a large baking sheet. Drizzle evenly with 2 tablespoons of the olive oil and sprinkle with the salt. Turn and drizzle with the remaining 2 tablespoons olive oil. Top with the thyme and place in the oven. Cook until lightly browned, about 10 minutes. Turn and cook until lightly browned on the second side, 5–6 minutes longer. Place under a preheated broiler (griller) until a slightly golden crust forms on the tops of the slices, 2–3 minutes. Turn and broil (grill) on the second side until golden, 2–3 minutes longer.

❋ Reduce the oven temperature to 400°F (200°C).

❋ Arrange one-third of the eggplant slices in a shallow 2-qt (2-l) baking dish. Top with layers of sauce, mozzarella, oregano, and Parmesan. Repeat the layers, beginning with the eggplant. Reserve a layer of egg-plant, sauce, and then Parmesan for the top. Dot evenly with the butter.

❋ Bake for 15 minutes. Remove the dish from the oven and carefully tip it, pressing on the surface with a spoon or spatula. If there seems to be too much juice, pour off the excess. Return to the oven and cook until the top is lightly browned and bubbling, 15–20 minutes longer. Remove from the oven, cover loosely with aluminum foil, and let stand for 10 minutes. Scoop from the dish to serve.

NUTRITIONAL ANALYSIS PER SERVING: Calories 441 (Kilojoules 1,852); Protein 15 g; Carbohydrates 37 g; Total Fat 30 g; Saturated Fat 10 g; Cholesterol 39 mg; Sodium 493 mg; Dietary Fiber 9 g

Green Tomato and Fresh Corn Pie

PREP TIME: 40 MINUTES

COOKING TIME: 40 MINUTES

INGREDIENTS

FOR THE FILLING

⅓ lb (155 g) spicy chicken sausages

½ yellow onion, minced

1 red bell pepper (capsicum), seeded
and minced

1 jalapeño, Hungarian wax, or serrano
chile, seeded and minced

kernels from 2 ears of corn

12 tart green or black olives, pitted
and coarsely chopped

¼ cup (1½ oz/45 g) all-purpose
(plain) flour

2 tablespoons fine cornmeal

½ teaspoon salt

½ teaspoon ground pepper

4 or 5 large green tomatoes, chopped

1½ tablespoons unsalted butter

2 tablespoons vegetable oil

FOR THE TOPPING

¾ cup (4 oz/125 g) fine cornmeal

2 tablespoons all-purpose (plain) flour

2 tablespoons fresh thyme leaves

1 teaspoon baking powder

½ teaspoon salt

½ teaspoon ground pepper

2 eggs, beaten

½ cup (4 fl oz/125 ml) milk

1 tablespoon vegetable oil

This easy-to-assemble, home-style dish makes for convenient outdoor entertaining. Yellow or white corn, or a combination, can be used.

SERVES 4–6

❋ Preheat an oven to 425°F (220°C). Butter a shallow 1½-qt (1.5-l) baking dish.

❋ To make the filling, remove the sausages from the casings. In a frying pan over medium heat, cook the sausages, using a wooden spoon to stir often and break up the meat, until cooked through and somewhat crumbly, about 5 minutes. Transfer to paper towels to drain. Pour off any excess fat, leaving a scant ½ teaspoon. Return the pan to medium heat and add the onion, bell pepper, and chile. Cook, stirring often, until the vegetables begin to soften, 3–4 minutes. Transfer to a bowl, add the sausage, corn kernels, and olives, and stir to mix. Set aside.

❋ In a bowl, stir together the flour, cornmeal, salt, and pepper. Add the green tomatoes and turn to coat with the flour mixture. In a sauté pan over medium-high heat, melt the butter with the oil. When the butter foams, use a slotted spoon to transfer the tomatoes to the sauté pan. Do not add the accumulated juices in the bottom of the bowl. Cook, stirring, until the tomatoes have browned slightly, 3–4 minutes. Turn and cook until golden brown, 2–3 minutes longer. Transfer to a plate and set aside.

❋ To make the topping, in a bowl, stir together the cornmeal, flour, thyme, baking powder, salt, and pepper. Stir in the eggs, milk, and oil and mix just until thoroughly moistened.

❋ Pour the sausage mixture into the prepared dish, spreading evenly. Top with the green tomatoes, again spreading evenly. Pour the topping evenly over the tomatoes.

❋ Bake until the topping is slightly puffed and cooked throughout, 15–20 minutes. Remove from the oven, cover loosely with aluminum foil, and let stand for 10–15 minutes. Scoop from the dish to serve.

NUTRITIONAL ANALYSIS PER SERVING: Calories 378 (Kilojoules 1,588); Protein 9 g; Carbohydrates 44 g; Total Fat 19 g; Saturated Fat 5 g; Cholesterol 98 mg; Sodium 871 mg; Dietary Fiber 4 g

Foil-Wrapped Stuffed Pork Chops

PREP TIME: 45 MINUTES

COOKING TIME: 55 MINUTES

INGREDIENTS

FOR THE STUFFING

2½ cups (5 oz/155 g) cubed day-old bread (1-inch/2.5-cm cubes), preferably coarse country bread

1–2 cups (8–16 fl oz/250–500 ml) milk

3 tablespoons minced yellow onion

2 tablespoons chopped fresh parsley

1 tablespoon minced fresh sage

2 teaspoons minced fresh thyme

1 teaspoon dried winter savory

½ teaspoon salt

½ teaspoon ground pepper

4 large loin pork chops, each about 10 oz (315 g) and 1½ inches (4 cm) thick

½ teaspoon salt

½ teaspoon ground pepper

SERVING TIP: The packets are full of steam, so diners should be careful when opening them not to be burned by the escaping steam. Also in the packet are the flavorful juices collected during cooking, which should not be lost.

When the sealed packets are unfolded at the table, each guest is greeted with an aromatic prelude to the herb-infused chops. Vegetables such as green bell peppers (capsicums), tomato halves, or sections of corn on the cob can be added to the foil packet, making it a one-dish meal. Serve with lots of crusty bread for dipping into the juices.

SERVES 4

❀ Preheat an oven to 350°F (180°C).

❀ To make the stuffing, place the bread cubes in a bowl and pour in 1 cup (8 fl oz/250 ml) of the milk. Let stand until the bread is very soft and has absorbed the milk, about 15 minutes. This timing will depend upon the kind of bread and how dry it is. If necessary, add up to 1 cup (8 fl oz/250 ml) more milk. When the bread is ready, squeeze dry and place in a clean bowl. Discard the milk. Add the onion, parsley, sage, thyme, winter savory, salt, and pepper to the bread and mix well.

❀ Using a small, sharp knife, cut a horizontal slit 1 inch (2.5 cm) long into the side of each pork chop. Working inward from the slit, cut almost to the opposite side of the chop; be careful not to cut through the chop completely. Spoon an equal amount of the stuffing into each chop. They will be quite full.

❀ Sprinkle the salt into a wide, heavy frying pan and place over medium-high heat. When it is hot, add the pork chops and sear, turning once, until nicely browned on both sides, about 2 minutes on each side.

❀ Cut 4 pieces of aluminum foil each large enough to wrap and seal a pork chop. Place a chop on each piece of foil, sprinkle with the pepper, and then fold in the ends of the foil, overlapping them. Bring the sides together and fold over to make a tight seal. Place on a baking sheet and bake for 45–50 minutes. To test for doneness, open 1 foil packet and check that the stuffing is cooked through and the pork is opaque when cut into with a knife. Do not overcook or the pork will be dry.

❀ To serve, place the packets on 4 individual plates and let diners open them at the table.

NUTRITIONAL ANALYSIS PER SERVING: Calories 597 (Kilojoules 2,507); Protein 50 g; Carbohydrates 24 g; Total Fat 32 g; Saturated Fat 12 g; Cholesterol 152 mg; Sodium 919 mg; Dietary Fiber 1 g

Leg of Lamb with Lemon-Bay Marinade

PREP TIME: 15 MINUTES, PLUS
12 HOURS FOR MARINATING

COOKING TIME: 35 MINUTES,
PLUS PREPARING FIRE

INGREDIENTS

⅔ cup (5 fl oz/160 ml) olive oil

juice of 3 lemons, plus 3 lemons,
thinly sliced

8 cloves garlic, bruised

2 bay leaves

2 tablespoons fresh thyme leaves or
8 thyme sprigs, each 6 inches
(15 cm) long

2 tablespoons peppercorns, bruised

2 tablespoons coriander seeds,
bruised

1½ teaspoons salt

1 leg of lamb, 6–7 lb (3–3.5 kg),
boned and butterflied

PREP TIP: To bruise whole spices, put
them in a mortar and gently tap with
a heavy pestle to break their surfaces
slightly. Or place in a heavy-duty
plastic bag, set on a work surface,
and then tap with a heavy frying pan.
To bruise garlic cloves, place on a
cutting board and crush with the
side of a chef's knife.

Marinated and grilled lamb is an easy main course to prepare
and serve outdoors, as it moves directly from the grill to the
table and your waiting guests.

SERVES 8–10

❋ In a shallow, nonaluminum dish or bowl large enough to hold the
lamb, combine the olive oil, lemon juice and lemon slices, garlic, bay
leaves, thyme, peppercorns, coriander seeds, and salt. Stir to mix well.
Add the lamb and turn to coat well. Cover and refrigerate for 12–24
hours, turning the lamb from time to time.

❋ Prepare a fire in a grill. When the coals are medium-hot, remove
the lamb from the marinade and place on the grill rack about 8 inches
(20 cm) above the fire. Grill until deeply browned on the first side,
about 10 minutes, being careful the meat does not burn. Turn and grill
until deeply browned on the second side, or until an instant-read thermometer inserted into the thickest part of the leg registers 135°F (57°C)
for medium-rare or 145°F (63°C) for medium, 20–25 minutes longer.
Transfer the lamb to a cutting board or platter and cover loosely with
aluminum foil. Let rest for 10 minutes.

❋ To serve, cut the lamb across the grain into thin slices and arrange on
a warmed platter. Serve immediately, spooning some of the accumulated
juices over each portion.

NUTRITIONAL ANALYSIS PER SERVING: Calories 340 (Kilojoules 1,428); Protein 45 g;
Carbohydrates 1 g; Total Fat 16 g; Saturated Fat 5 g; Cholesterol 140 mg; Sodium 200 mg;
Dietary Fiber 0 g

Chicken in Green Mole

PREP TIME: 50 MINUTES

COOKING TIME: 1¼ HOURS

INGREDIENTS

5 chicken breast halves, ½ lb (250 g)
  each

12 chicken thighs, ½ lb (250 g) each

1 yellow onion, halved

1 piece peeled fresh ginger, about
  1 inch (2.5 cm)

2½ teaspoons salt, plus salt to taste

1 teaspoon peppercorns

4 Anaheim or poblano chiles

2 serrano chiles

5 tomatillos, husks removed

2 tablespoons vegetable oil

1 tablespoon shelled pumpkin seeds

10 blanched almonds

2 teaspoons sesame seeds

½ yellow onion, coarsely chopped

1 green bell pepper (capsicum),
  quartered lengthwise and seeded

1 tomato, seeded and chopped

2 cloves garlic, chopped

1 tablespoon unsalted peanut butter

2 whole allspice berries

1 large head romaine (cos) lettuce,
  coarsely chopped

1 cup (1 oz/30 g) fresh parsley leaves

1 corn tortilla, torn into pieces, if
  needed

¼ cup (¼ oz/7 g) fresh cilantro
  (fresh coriander) leaves

This version of green mole, or *mole verde,* acquires its characteristic bright color from romaine lettuce and Anaheim chiles and its thick texture from seeds and nuts. Accompany with rice and corn tortillas.

SERVES 10

✳ Put all the chicken pieces in a large, heavy saucepan. Add water just to cover and the onion, ginger, 1 teaspoon of the salt, and peppercorns. Bring to a boil, skimming any foam that rises to the surface. Reduce the heat to low, cover, and simmer until the chicken is tender and the juices run clear when a thigh is pierced, about 40 minutes. Transfer the chicken pieces to a baking dish and cover to keep warm. Using a large spoon, skim off the fat from the stock; reserve the stock.

✳ Meanwhile, preheat a broiler (griller). Place the chiles and tomatillos on a broiler pan and slip under the broiler. Broil (grill), turning as needed, just until the skins are evenly blackened and blistered. Place on a plate, cover with aluminum foil, and let stand 10 minutes. Peel away the skins from the chiles, then cut in half lengthwise, remove the seeds, and coarsely chop the chiles. Cut the tomatillos into quarters. In a blender or food processor, combine the chiles and tomatillos with 1 cup (8 fl oz/ 250 ml) of the reserved stock. Purée until smooth.

✳ In a sauté pan over medium heat, warm the vegetable oil. Add the pumpkin seeds and almonds and sauté until lightly golden, 3–4 minutes. Add the sesame seeds and sauté for 2 minutes longer. Transfer to the chile mixture along with the onion, bell pepper, tomato, garlic, peanut butter, allspice, remaining 1½ teaspoons salt, and ½ cup (4 fl oz/125 ml) of the reserved stock. Purée until smooth. Add the lettuce and parsley and process again. The mixture should be thick, not watery. If it is too thick, thin with a little more stock; if too thin, add the tortilla pieces and process until thickened. Taste and add salt if needed.

✳ Transfer the sauce to a saucepan and place over low heat. Cook until the color changes from a bright to a darker green, 10–15 minutes. Remove the skin from the chicken and transfer to a serving platter. Pour the hot sauce over the chicken, garnish with the cilantro, and serve.

NUTRITIONAL ANALYSIS PER SERVING: Calories 425 (Kilojoules 1,785); Protein 51 g; Carbohydrates 9 g; Total Fat 20 g; Saturated Fat 5 g; Cholesterol 158 mg; Sodium 715 mg; Dietary Fiber 2 g

Vegetable Rice Bake – *Serves 6*

3 cups cooked brown rice
3 tbsp **Cha-Cha Chinese Chicken Salad Dressing**
1 tbsp soy sauce
1 cup each: broccoli flowerets, small mushroom caps, red bell pepper cubes, sliced carrots and sliced celery
1 cup shredded sharp cheddar cheese
2 tbsp roasted sunflower seed kernels

In a large casserole dish combine rice, **Cha-Cha Chinese Chicken Salad Dressing** and soy sauce; stir well. Meanwhile, lightly steam vegetables until crisp-tender. Do not over cook. Place vegetables on top of rice and sprinkle with cheese. Top with sunflower seeds. Bake at 400°F until cheese is melted and mixture is heated through.

Try our other products: Chinese Marinade, Veri Veri Teriyaki and Island Teriyaki!

Spicy Bow Tie Salad – *Serves 4-6*

8 oz bow tie pasta, cooked al dente and drained
1/2 cup **Cha-Cha Chinese Chicken Salad Dressing**
1/3 cup shredded purple cabbage
1-1/4 cup green peas
1/4 cup peanuts
1 tbsp rice vinegar
1/2 tsp hot chili oil

Combine all ingredients in a large bowl; toss well to mix and to coat with dressing. Chill well. Mix again before serving.

ooms

alf cooked.
ntil mush-
g bowl with
zer or as a

l to
Mix

Smoked Pork Loin with Red Onion Confit

PREP TIME: 20 MINUTES

COOKING TIME: 2 HOURS,
    PLUS PREPARING FIRE

INGREDIENTS

⅓ cup (⅓ oz/10 g) fresh rosemary
    leaves, plus 12 fresh rosemary
    branches, each 14–16 inches
    (35–40 cm) long

⅓ cup (⅓ oz/10 g) chopped fresh
    sage

1 teaspoon coarse sea salt

6 peppercorns

2 tablespoons olive oil

1 boneless pork loin, 4½ lb (2.25 kg)

FOR THE CONFIT

¼ cup (2 oz/60 g) unsalted butter,
    cut into pieces

4 lb (2 kg) red (Spanish) onions,
    thickly sliced

2 bay leaves

2 tablespoons fresh thyme leaves

1 tablespoon fresh winter savory
    leaves or ½ teaspoon dried winter
    savory

1 teaspoon ground pepper

½ teaspoon salt

¼ cup (2 fl oz/60 ml) olive oil

Long, slow cooking in a kettle-type grill smokes the pork to perfection and infuses it with the earthy fragrance of rosemary.

SERVES 10–12

✳ Place the rosemary leaves, chopped sage, sea salt, and peppercorns in a spice grinder and grind coarsely. Transfer to a small bowl, add 1 tablespoon of the olive oil, and stir to make a paste. Rub the pork loin with the remaining 1 tablespoon olive oil and then rub with the paste.

✳ Using 60–70 charcoal briquettes, prepare a fire in a kettle grill with a vented bottom and a fitted, vented lid. When the coals are hot, spread over the bottom of the grill and add another 12 briquettes. Let burn for 2–3 minutes, then close the bottom vent. Place the pork loin on the grill rack 8–10 inches (20–25 cm) above the fire. Cover and open the lid vent fully. Cook for 15 minutes, then turn and cook for another 15 minutes. Remove the pork loin from the grill and lay the rosemary branches on the rack to form a bed. Place the roast on the branches, cover the grill, and open the bottom vent. Let the smoke rise in a steady stream through the lid vent for about 5 minutes, then close the bottom vent. Cook for 10 minutes, then again open the bottom vent about ¼ inch (6 mm). Continue to grill, turning the loin every 15 minutes, until an instant-read thermometer registers 170°F (77°C), about 1¼ hours longer. Transfer to a cutting board, cover loosely with aluminum foil, and let stand for 10–15 minutes before slicing.

✳ Meanwhile, prepare the onion confit: Preheat an oven to 300°F (150°C). Place the butter on a large baking sheet and melt in the oven, 4–5 minutes. Remove and spread the onions on the baking sheet to make a layer about 1 inch (2.5 cm) deep. Add the bay leaves, thyme, savory, pepper, and salt. Drizzle evenly with the olive oil. Bake the onions, turning every 10–15 minutes, until light golden brown and reduced in volume by nearly half, about 1½ hours.

✳ Thinly slice the pork. Spoon the onion confit on individual plates and top with the pork. Serve hot or at room temperature.

NUTRITIONAL ANALYSIS PER SERVING: Calories 524 (Kilojoules 2,201); Protein 28 g; Carbohydrates 16 g; Total Fat 39 g; Saturated Fat 14 g; Cholesterol 113 mg; Sodium 323 mg; Dietary Fiber 3 g

Ragout of Spring Vegetables with Almond Couscous

PREP TIME: 35 MINUTES

COOKING TIME: 1¼ HOURS

INGREDIENTS

FOR THE RAGOUT

12 baby turnips, trimmed, with ½ inch (12 mm) of stem intact

1½ lb (750 g) fava (broad) beans, shelled

1½ lb (750 g) peas, shelled

¼ cup (2 oz/60 g) unsalted butter

½ cup (2½ oz/75 g) chopped shallots

1 cup (8 fl oz/250 ml) dry white wine

3 cups (24 fl oz/750 ml) vegetable or chicken broth

18 small new potatoes

2 teaspoons ground pepper

1 teaspoon salt, plus salt to taste

18 baby carrots, peeled

½ cup (1½ oz/45 g) chopped tender leek greens, plus 8 small leeks, white part only, cut into 2-inch (5-cm) lengths

¼ cup (⅓ oz/10 g) finely snipped fresh chives

2 tablespoons minced fresh tarragon

2 tablespoons minced fresh parsley

FOR THE COUSCOUS

½ cup (2¼ oz/67 g) slivered blanched almonds

scant 2 cups (16 fl oz/500 ml) water

1 tablespoon butter

½ teaspoon salt

2 cups (12 oz/375 g) instant couscous

This stew, using the first vegetables of spring, is a seasonal celebration of the garden.

SERVES 6

✸ Place the turnips on a steamer rack over boiling water, cover, and steam until tender, 8–10 minutes. Set aside. Bring a saucepan three-fourths full of water to a boil and add the fava beans. Boil for 30 seconds, drain, and rinse with cold running water. Slit the thin skin surrounding each bean and slip it off. Place the favas and peas on the steamer rack over boiling water, cover, and steam until tender, 6–7 minutes.

✸ In a large, heavy saucepan over medium-high heat, melt the butter until foamy. Add the shallots and sauté until translucent, 6–7 minutes. Pour in the white wine and deglaze the pan, stirring to dislodge any browned bits from the pan bottom. Add the broth, potatoes, pepper, and 1 teaspoon salt. Cover tightly, reduce the heat to medium-low, and simmer for 10 minutes. Stir in the carrots and leek greens and arrange the white parts of the leeks on top. Cover and cook until the carrots and potatoes are almost tender, 8–10 minutes longer. Add the turnips, peas, and favas, turning them gently in the simmering stew. Re-cover and cook until all the vegetables are tender, 6–7 minutes longer. Season to taste with salt. Stir in all but about 1 teaspoon each of the chives, tarragon, and parsley.

✸ Meanwhile, make the couscous: Preheat an oven to 450°F (230°C). Butter an ovenproof 3-cup (24–fl oz/750-ml) mold. Spread the almonds on a baking sheet and toast, stirring often, until golden and fragrant, 7–8 minutes. Transfer to the bottom of the prepared mold. Reduce the oven temperature to 350°F (180°C). In a saucepan, combine the water, butter, and salt and bring to a boil. Pour in the couscous and return to a boil. Immediately remove from the heat, cover, and let stand for 5 minutes. Fluff with a fork, then pack into the mold and place in the oven until set, about 10 minutes.

✸ To serve, invert a serving plate over the top of the mold, then invert the plate and mold together; lift off the mold. Spoon the ragout around the couscous or serve separately in a warmed dish. Garnish with the remaining herbs.

NUTRITIONAL ANALYSIS PER SERVING: Calories 700 (Kilojoules 2,940); Protein 21 g; Carbohydrates 118 g; Total Fat 17 g; Saturated Fat 7 g; Cholesterol 26 mg; Sodium 1,252 mg; Dietary Fiber 12 g

Poached Salmon with Green Grape Sauce

PREP TIME: 20 MINUTES

COOKING TIME: 10 MINUTES

INGREDIENTS

FOR THE SAUCE

½ cup (2 oz/60 g) fine dried bread
crumbs

½ cup (2½ oz/75 g) almonds

2 cloves garlic, chopped

2 tablespoons chopped fresh parsley

I teaspoon sugar

½ teaspoon salt

½ teaspoon ground pepper

I cup (8 fl oz/250 ml) juice from
unripe or sour grapes, strained

¼ cup (2 fl oz/60 ml) chicken broth

FOR THE SALMON

2 bunches fresh tarragon

I teaspoon salt

2 lemons, sliced

4 salmon fillets, each about ¼ lb
(125 g) and ½ inch (12 mm) thick

2 cups (3 oz/90 g) mixed young
salad greens

PREP TIP: To juice unripe or sour
grapes, pit them in a mortar and crush
with a pestle, or pass them through a
food mill. Strain the juice to remove
any skins and seeds.

The fresh juice of the underripe grapes of early summer, also known as verjuice, is combined with ground almonds, broth, and seasonings for a distinctive sauce. If underripe grapes or bottled verjuice is unavailable, substitute fresh lime juice for a slightly different version of the sauce.

SERVES 4

❋ To make the sauce, in a blender or food processor, combine the bread crumbs, almonds, garlic, parsley, sugar, salt, and pepper. Purée until nearly smooth. With the motor running, add the grape juice in a slow, steady stream, processing until a smooth paste forms. Set the grape juice mixture aside. Pour the chicken broth into a small saucepan and set aside as well.

❋ To cook the salmon, pour water to a depth of 3 inches (7.5 cm) into a wide, deep sauté pan or saucepan just large enough to hold the salmon fillets in a single layer. Add the tarragon, salt, and lemon slices to the water. Place over high heat, cover, and bring to just below a boil so that the water shimmers with movement but does not bubble. Slip the fillets into the water and poach, uncovered, until the flesh just easily flakes with a fork, about 7 minutes.

❋ Meanwhile, place the saucepan holding the broth over medium heat, bring to a simmer, and stir in the grape juice mixture. Heat, stirring occasionally, until hot. Do not allow to boil or scorch.

❋ Using a spatula, transfer the salmon fillets to 4 individual plates. Garnish the plates with the salad greens, then spoon 2 or 3 tablespoons of warm sauce over each salmon fillet and serve. Pass the remaining sauce in a warmed bowl at the table.

NUTRITIONAL ANALYSIS PER SERVING: Calories 353 (Kilojoules 1,483); Protein 29 g; Carbohydrates 22 g; Total Fat 17 g; Saturated Fat 2 g; Cholesterol 62 mg; Sodium 646 mg; Dietary Fiber 3 g

French-Style Steaks and Skewers of Rosemary-Scented Morels

PREP TIME: 15 MINUTES

COOKING TIME: 15 MINUTES,
    PLUS PREPARING FIRE

INGREDIENTS

24 fresh morel mushrooms, brushed
    clean

1 teaspoon ground pepper, plus
    pepper to taste

¾ teaspoon salt, plus salt to taste

2 tablespoons unsalted butter, cut
    into bits

4 fresh rosemary branches, each
    about 8 inches (20 cm) long

4 boneless rib-eye steaks, each
    about ⅓ lb (155 g) and ½ inch
    (12 mm) thick

PREP TIP: If fresh morels are
unavailable, dried morels may be
used. First put them in a bowl and
add hot water to cover. Soak for
20 minutes, then drain and pat
dry. Fresh shiitake mushrooms
can also be substituted.

Boneless slices of rib-eye steak make an excellent choice to accompany woodsy morel mushrooms. The mushrooms are threaded on wooden or metal skewers and laid atop a bed of rosemary branches to grill. If desired, use 8 rosemary branches in place of the skewers and soak in water to cover for 20–30 minutes before threading three mushrooms on each branch.

SERVES 4

❊ Prepare a fire in a grill.

❊ Thread the morels onto 4 skewers, dividing them evenly. (If using wooden skewers, first soak in water to cover for 20–30 minutes.) Sprinkle the mushrooms with the 1 teaspoon pepper and the ¼ teaspoon salt and dot with the butter. Lay a 12-inch (30-cm) square of heavy-duty aluminum foil on a work surface and place the rosemary branches on it in a single layer. Top each length of rosemary with a skewer.

❊ When the coals are medium-hot, place the skewer-topped aluminum foil on the grill rack and grill, turning the skewers often, just until the mushrooms are cooked through, 3–4 minutes. Remove from the grill and discard the rosemary branches. Roll each skewer in the buttery juices that have accumulated on the foil before serving. Keep warm until the steaks are grilled.

❊ Place the steaks on the rack over hot coals and grill, turning once, for 2–3 minutes on each side for medium-rare, 3–5 minutes on each side for medium. Season with salt and pepper and transfer to 4 individual plates. Top each steak with a morel skewer and serve.

NUTRITIONAL ANALYSIS PER SERVING: Calories 427 (Kilojoules 1,793); Protein 30 g; Carbohydrates 4 g; Total Fat 31 g; Saturated Fat 14 g; Cholesterol 109 mg; Sodium 485 mg; Dietary Fiber 0 g

Double-Corn and Chile Spoon Bread

PREP TIME: 25 MINUTES

COOKING TIME: 35 MINUTES

INGREDIENTS

6 large Anaheim or other mild green
  chiles

2 bacon slices, cut into 1-inch
  (2.5-cm) pieces

½ cup (2 oz/60 g) shredded Monterey
  jack cheese

½ cup (2 oz/60 g) shredded sharp
  cheddar cheese

3 eggs, separated

kernels from 3 ears of white or
  yellow corn

⅓ cup (3 fl oz/80 ml) milk

2 tablespoons sour cream

2 tablespoons fine yellow cornmeal

2 tablespoons all-purpose (plain) flour

½ teaspoon salt

PREP TIP: To remove the kernels
from an ear of corn, hold the pointed
end and steady the stalk end on a
cutting board. Using a sturdy, sharp
knife, cut down and away from you
along the ear to strip off the kernels,
turning the ear slightly with each
new cut.

Light, fluffy spoon bread, reminiscent of a soufflé, is laced with
cheese, corn kernels, and green chiles to make a complete meal
when accompanied with a platter of sliced tomatoes and a
green salad.

SERVES 4–6

❀ Preheat a broiler (griller). Place the chiles on a broiler pan and slip
under the broiler. Broil (grill), turning as needed, just until the skins are
evenly blackened and blistered. Transfer the chiles to a plate, cover with
aluminum foil, and let stand for 10 minutes. Peel away the skins, then
cut the chiles in half lengthwise and remove and discard the seeds.

❀ Preheat an oven to 350°F (180°C).

❀ In a frying pan over medium heat, cook the bacon until barely
browned, 6–7 minutes. Transfer to paper towels to drain.

❀ Butter an 8-inch (20-cm) square baking dish. Layer the chiles in the
bottom of the prepared dish. Sprinkle evenly with the jack and cheddar
cheeses. In a bowl, beat the egg whites with an electric mixer until fluffy
but not stiff. In another, larger bowl, combine the egg yolks, corn kernels, milk, sour cream, cornmeal, flour, and salt. Using a fork, beat until
blended. Using a rubber spatula, gently fold the egg whites into the
cornmeal mixture. Spoon the egg mixture evenly over the cheese and
chiles. Scatter the bacon pieces over the top.

❀ Bake the spoon bread until it is set around the sides but still jiggles
slightly in the center when the pan is gently shaken, about 20 minutes.
Scoop from the dish to serve.

NUTRITIONAL ANALYSIS PER SERVING: Calories 275 (Kilojoules 1,155); Protein 14 g;
Carbohydrates 23 g; Total Fat 15 g; Saturated Fat 8 g; Cholesterol 160 mg; Sodium 460 mg;
Dietary Fiber 3 g

Mixed Sausages and Eggplant Grill

PREP TIME: 10 MINUTES

COOKING TIME: 30 MINUTES,
    PLUS PREPARING FIRE

INGREDIENTS

2 or 3 eggplants (aubergines), cut
    crosswise into slices ½ inch
    (12 mm) thick

¼ cup (2 fl oz/60 ml) olive oil

1 tablespoon fresh thyme leaves

1 teaspoon ground pepper

¼ teaspoon salt

12–18 assorted sausages, 3–4½ lb
    (1.5–2.25 kg) total weight, such as
    mild Italian, chicken-apple, or
    bratwurst

SERVING TIP: Offer split French rolls
or sections of a baguette loaf, and
invite guests to assemble their own
sausage-and-eggplant sandwiches.

Hearty flavors and simple preparation make this a good dish to
serve to a crowd. The eggplant can be marinated in the oil and
seasonings up to 1 hour in advance of grilling.

SERVES 6–8

⊛ Prepare a fire in a grill.

⊛ Brush the eggplant slices on both sides with the olive oil. Place in a
bowl or shallow baking dish. Add the thyme, pepper, and salt and toss
to distribute evenly.

⊛ When the coals are medium-hot, place the eggplant slices directly on
the grill rack or in a grill basket on the rack. Grill until a golden crust
forms on the first side, 7–8 minutes. Turn and grill on the second side
until a golden crust forms, 6–7 minutes longer. Transfer to a platter
and keep warm or let cool to room temperature.

⊛ Arrange the sausages on the grill rack or in a grill basket on the rack.
Grill, turning often, until the juices run clear when the sausages are
pierced, 10–15 minutes. Remove the sausages from the grill and arrange
on one or more platters with the eggplant slices.

NUTRITIONAL ANALYSIS PER SERVING: Calories 735 (Kilojoules 3,087); Protein 38 g;
Carbohydrates 16 g; Total Fat 58 g; Saturated Fat 18 g; Cholesterol 123 mg; Sodium 1,649 mg;
Dietary Fiber 3 g

Filo Ice-Cream Cups with Summer Fruit

PREP TIME: 25 MINUTES

COOKING TIME: 10 MINUTES

INGREDIENTS

4 sheets filo dough, each about 12 by 16 inches (30 by 40 cm), thawed if frozen

¼ cup (2 oz/60 g) unsalted butter, melted

2 qt (2 l) strawberry ice cream

2 cups (8 oz/250 g) sliced strawberries

whipped cream (optional)

sliced peaches (optional)

PREP TIP: Filo dough can be purchased in the frozen-food section of most food stores and specialty markets. As you work with it, keep the unused portion covered with a moist kitchen towel at all times. Even a few minutes of exposure to air can dry out the dough and make it brittle.

For a fun, unfussy finale to an outdoor party, fill baked filo dough cups with strawberry ice cream and sliced fresh strawberries. Other ice cream and fruit combinations, such as vanilla with peaches or apricots, can be used.

SERVES 12

❋ Preheat an oven to 325°F (165°C).

❋ Butter 12 standard muffin cups. Lay 1 filo sheet on a piece of waxed paper or aluminum foil. Brush thoroughly with some of the melted butter. Top with the remaining 3 sheets, brushing each one with some of the butter. Cut the stack of sheets into pieces about 4 inches (10 cm) square so you have 12 layered squares in all. Tuck each layered square into a prepared muffin cup, pressing it in gently with your fingertips.

❋ Bake until the cups are crisp and golden, about 10 minutes. Remove from the oven and let stand until cool enough to handle. Remove from the muffin cups and let cool completely on racks.

❋ Just before serving, place the cups on 12 dessert plates. Fill each cup with a scoop of ice cream and top with sliced strawberries. Garnish with a dollop of whipped cream and a peach slice, if desired.

NUTRITIONAL ANALYSIS PER SERVING: Calories 229 (Kilojoules 962); Protein 3 g; Carbohydrates 29 g; Total Fat 12 g; Saturated Fat 2 g; Cholesterol 36 mg; Sodium 123 mg; Dietary Fiber 1 g

Fresh Cherry Pie

PREP TIME: 30 MINUTES

COOKING TIME: 40 MINUTES,
    PLUS 15 MINUTES FOR
    COOLING

INGREDIENTS

FOR THE PASTRY

2 cups (10 oz/315 g) all-purpose
    (plain) flour

1 teaspoon salt

½ cup (4 oz/125 g) unsalted butter,
    at room temperature, cut into bits

5–6 tablespoons (3 fl oz/90 ml) ice
    water

FOR THE FILLING

1 lb (500 g) sweet or sour cherries,
    pitted *(see note)*

½ cup (4 oz/125 g) sugar

¼ cup (1½ oz/45 g) all-purpose (plain)
    flour

1 tablespoon unsalted butter, cut
    into bits

PREP TIP: A cherry pitter, a simple
device with a plunger that forces
out the pit, will simplify the pitting
process. Some models call for load-
ing the cherries individually, while
others have a hamper that releases
the cherries one by one as the
plunger is depressed.

Pies are easy to serve at an outdoor party. Home-made cherry
pie is one of the great treats of late spring and early summer.
Sour cherries such as Montmorency or Morello will result in a
sharp-sweet flavor, while Bings, Tartarians, or Royal Anns will
make a sweeter pie.

SERVES 6

❊ Preheat an oven to 425°F (220°C).

❊ To make the pastry, sift the flour into a bowl, then resift with the salt.
Put the flour into a food processor, then add the butter. Process until
pea-sized pieces form, 1–2 minutes. Add the ice water and process until
the dough gathers together into a ball.

❊ Remove the dough from the processor and divide roughly in half,
with 1 portion slightly larger than the other. On a floured work surface,
roll out the larger portion into a round about 10 inches (25 cm) in diameter and ⅛ inch (3 mm) thick. Drape the round over the rolling pin and
carefully transfer to an 8-inch (20-cm) pie pan. Gently ease the dough
round into the pan. Trim the overhang to ½ inch (12 mm).

❊ To make the filling, place the cherries in a bowl. In a small bowl, stir
together the sugar and flour, then add to the cherries. Turn the cherries
to coat with the sugar mixture. Transfer the filling to the pastry-lined
pie pan, mounding it slightly in the center. Dot with the butter.

❊ On the floured work surface, roll out the remaining dough portion
into a round about 9 inches (23 cm) in diameter and ⅛ inch (3 mm)
thick. Carefully place over the cherries and trim the overhang to 1 inch
(2.5 cm). Fold the top crust edge under the bottom crust edge; press to
seal and crimp decoratively. Cut several slits in the top crust. Place the
pie on a baking sheet.

❊ Bake for 15 minutes. Reduce the oven temperature to 350°F (180°C)
and continue to bake until the cherries are soft when pierced through
one of the slits and a syrup has formed, 20–25 minutes longer. Remove
from the oven and let cool for at least 15 minutes before serving.

NUTRITIONAL ANALYSIS PER SERVING: Calories 437 (Kilojoules 1,835); Protein 6 g;
Carbohydrates 64 g; Total Fat 18 g; Saturated Fat 11 g; Cholesterol 47 mg; Sodium 544 mg;
Dietary Fiber 2 g

Free-Form Pear Tart

PREP TIME: 25 MINUTES

COOKING TIME: 30 MINUTES

INGREDIENTS

3 or 4 firm but ripe pears such as
   Bosc, Anjou, or Comice, peeled,
   cored, and sliced

¼ cup (2 oz/60 g) sugar

1 tablespoon all-purpose (plain) flour

2 tablespoons lemon juice

1 lb (500 g) frozen puff pastry,
   thawed in the refrigerator

1 tablespoon unsalted butter, cut
   into bits

PREP TIP: The easiest way to core
pears is to quarter them lengthwise,
then use a small, sharp knife to cut
the core sections from each piece.

A simple tart is the essence of light, outdoor dessert fare. Other seasonal fruits—sliced plums, seedless grapes, sliced nectarines or peaches, boysenberries, or raspberries—can be used alone or in combination.

SERVES 6–8

❊ Preheat an oven to 400°F (200°C).

❊ In a bowl, combine the pears, sugar, and flour and toss to mix well. Add the lemon juice and stir to moisten evenly.

❊ On a floured work surface, roll out the puff pastry into a round about 15 inches (38 cm) in diameter. Transfer to an ungreased baking sheet. Spoon the fruit into the center of the round, leaving a 1½-inch (4-cm) border uncovered around the perimeter. The fruit will be stacked high, but it reduces as it cooks. Fold the edge of the pastry up to create a rim, pinching and tucking it as necessary. Dot the fruit with the butter.

❊ Bake until the pastry is puffed and golden brown, about 30 minutes. Do not undercook; use a spatula to lift the tart and check that the bottom is also golden brown.

❊ Cut into wedges and serve hot or at room temperature.

NUTRITIONAL ANALYSIS PER SERVING: Calories 451 (Kilojoules 1,894); Protein 5 g; Carbohydrates 49 g; Total Fat 27 g; Saturated Fat 5 g; Cholesterol 4 mg; Sodium 163 mg; Dietary Fiber 3 g

Strawberries in Red Wine with Vanilla Bean

PREP TIME: 20 MINUTES, PLUS
6 HOURS FOR MARINATING

INGREDIENTS

2 pt (1 lb/500 g) small or medium
   strawberries

¼–½ cup (2–4 oz/60–125 g) sugar

2 cups (16 fl oz/500 ml) dry red wine
   such as a Merlot or Zinfandel

1 vanilla bean (pod), split in half
   lengthwise

PREP TIP: Look for vanilla beans
imported from Madagascar, which
reputedly have the best flavor. Use a
sharp knife to split the bean in half.

Sweet and juicy on their own, fresh strawberries take on another flavor dimension in this simple, elegant French dessert. The vanilla bean can be omitted, if desired.

SERVES 6

❋ Hull the strawberries. Then, if they have a white core, cut it away with the tip of a sharp knife. Slice some of the larger berries in half, but leave most of the berries whole.

❋ Combine all the berries in a nonaluminum bowl, sprinkle with the sugar to taste, and then add the wine and vanilla bean. Cover and refrigerate for at least 6 hours or for up to 24 hours.

❋ Spoon into 6 glass bowls, lightly sprinkle with sugar, if desired, and serve cold.

NUTRITIONAL ANALYSIS PER SERVING: Calories 129 (Kilojoules 542); Protein 1 g; Carbohydrates 19 g; Total Fat 0 g; Saturated Fat 0 g; Cholesterol 0 mg; Sodium 5 mg; Dietary Fiber 2 g

Nectarine-Blackberry Cobbler

PREP TIME: 25 MINUTES

COOKING TIME: 40 MINUTES

INGREDIENTS

1 pt (8 oz/250 g) blackberries

3 firm, ripe nectarines, pitted and
sliced to make about 2 cups
(12 oz/375 g)

1 teaspoon lemon juice

½ cup (4 oz/125 g) sugar

2 tablespoons all-purpose (plain)
flour

FOR THE CRUST

1 cup (5 oz/155 g) all-purpose
(plain) flour

1¼ teaspoons baking powder

½ teaspoon salt

¼ cup (2 oz/60 g) chilled unsalted
butter

¼ cup (2 fl oz/60 ml) milk

The tart, distinct flavors of nectarines and blackberries are combined under a shortcake crust. Use the ripest blackberries you can find to ensure a juicy cobbler. For an extra treat, serve with a scoop of vanilla ice cream.

SERVES 6

❊ Preheat an oven to 450°F (230°C).

❊ In a bowl, combine the blackberries and nectarines. Stir in the lemon juice. In a small bowl, stir together the sugar and flour, then sprinkle over the fruits. Turn the fruits in the sugar mixture, coating them evenly. Set aside.

❊ To make the crust, in a bowl, stir together the flour, baking powder, and salt. Add the butter and, using a pastry blender or two knives, cut the butter into the flour until pea-sized pieces form. You might want to finish this with your fingertips. Using a fork, gradually stir in the milk, mixing until the dough sticks together. Gather the dough into a ball and transfer to a floured work surface. Using your fingers, pat out the dough into a 9-inch (23-cm) square about ¼ inch (6 mm) thick.

❊ Gently turn the fruits and their juices into an 8-inch (20-cm) square baking pan with 2½-inch (6-cm) sides. Lay the dough across the top and trim away any excess.

❊ Bake for 20 minutes. Reduce the heat to 300°F (150°C) and continue to bake until the berries and nectarines are tender but not dissolved, about 15–20 minutes longer. To test, lift up a corner of the crust and taste a piece of the fruit.

❊ Remove from the oven and serve warm or at room temperature, scooped from the pan.

NUTRITIONAL ANALYSIS PER SERVING: Calories 277 (Kilojoules 1,163); Protein 4 g; Carbohydrates 48 g; Total Fat 9 g; Saturated Fat 5 g; Cholesterol 22 mg; Sodium 290 mg; Dietary Fiber 4 g

Cherry Clafouti

PREP TIME: 20 MINUTES

COOKING TIME: 35 MINUTES

INGREDIENTS

1 cup (8 fl oz/250 ml) milk

¼ cup (2 fl oz/60 ml) heavy (double)
cream

3 eggs

1 tablespoon vanilla extract (essence)

⅔ cup (3 oz/90 g) all-purpose (plain)
flour, sifted

¼ cup (2 oz/60 g) granulated sugar

½ teaspoon salt

1–1½ lb (500–750 g) sweet or
sour cherries, pitted

1 tablespoon confectioners' (icing)
sugar

PREP TIP: Pit the cherries inside a
plastic bag. The juice won't stain the
work surface, and the stems and pits
are easy to discard.

A clafouti is a traditional cherry pudding cake from the Limousin region of France. Today it is made with other fruits as well, including apricots, nectarines, and blackberries. The cake puffs in the oven as it bakes, but collapses almost immediately once removed.

SERVES 6–8

⊛ Preheat an oven to 350°F (180°C). Butter a shallow 2-qt (2-l) baking dish.

⊛ In a bowl, combine the milk, cream, eggs, vanilla, flour, granulated sugar, and salt. Using an electric mixer, beat until frothy, about 5 minutes.

⊛ Pour enough of the batter into the prepared baking dish to cover the bottom with a layer about ¼ inch (6 mm) deep. Put the dish in the preheated oven for 2 minutes. Remove from the oven. Cover the surface with the cherries in a single layer. Pour the remaining batter over the top. Continue to bake until puffed and brown and a knife inserted into the center comes out clean, 30–35 minutes.

⊛ Remove from the oven and serve hot or at room temperature. Sprinkle with the confectioners' sugar just before scooping from the dish.

NUTRITIONAL ANALYSIS PER SERVING: Calories 221 (Kilojoules 928); Protein 6 g; Carbohydrates 32 g; Total Fat 8 g; Saturated Fat 4 g; Cholesterol 109 mg; Sodium 209 mg; Dietary Fiber 1 g

Mixed Grilled Fruits with Crème Anglaise

PREP TIME: 20 MINUTES

COOKING TIME: 20 MINUTES,
PLUS PREPARING FIRE

INGREDIENTS

FOR THE CRÈME ANGLAISE

2 cups (16 fl oz/500 ml) milk

1 vanilla bean (pod), split in half
lengthwise

2 whole eggs, plus 2 egg yolks

¼ cup (2 oz/60 g) sugar

⅛ teaspoon salt

2 peaches

2 plums

2 nectarines

2 pears

¼ cup (2 oz/60 g) unsalted butter,
melted

COOKING TIP: If your crème anglaise
develops lumps, remove them easily
by pouring the custard through a
fine-mesh sieve as soon as it is
removed from the heat.

Peaches, pears, plums, and nectarines are good candidates for grilling over a charcoal fire. After the fruits are brushed with melted butter, then grilled for a few minutes, the natural sugars begin to caramelize from the heat. A spoonful or two of crème anglaise completes the dish. For a more rustic presentation, serve the grilled fruits without a sauce.

SERVES 6–8

✳ Prepare a fire in a grill.

✳ To make the crème anglaise, pour the milk into a nonaluminum bowl and place over (not touching) simmering water in a pan. Add the vanilla bean. Warm until small bubbles appear along the bowl edges. Meanwhile, in another bowl, using a fork, beat together the whole eggs and egg yolks until slightly blended, then beat in the sugar and salt. Slowly stir in the hot milk and vanilla bean. Return the mixture to the nonaluminum bowl and place over (not touching) gently boiling water in the pan. Cook, stirring constantly with a spoon, until a thick custard forms, 7–10 minutes. To test, dip the spoon into the custard and draw your finger across the back of the spoon; it should leave a path. Remove from the heat, remove and discard the vanilla bean, and keep the custard hot over the hot water in the pan. (Alternatively, let cool to room temperature, cover with plastic wrap placed directly on the surface, and refrigerate until chilled, about 2 hours. The custard will thicken upon cooling and chilling.) You should have about 2¼ cups (18 fl oz/560 ml) custard.

✳ To prepare the fruit, cut the peaches, plums, nectarines, and pears in half through their stem ends. Cut away the core from the pears and discard the pits from the other fruits. Place the fruits in a grill basket and brush well on all sides with the melted butter.

✳ When the coals are medium-hot, place the basket on the grill rack. Cook, turning once, until the fruits begin to soften and then brown, 3–4 minutes on the first side and slightly less on the second side. Transfer the fruits to a serving platter and serve with the crème anglaise on the side.

NUTRITIONAL ANALYSIS PER SERVING: Calories 242 (Kilojoules 1,016); Protein 6 g; Carbohydrates 29 g; Total Fat 12 g; Saturated Fat 6 g; Cholesterol 149 mg; Sodium 161 mg; Dietary Fiber 3 g

Raspberry Crepes with Ice Cream

PREP TIME: 20 MINUTES, PLUS
2 HOURS FOR CHILLING

COOKING TIME: 20 MINUTES

INGREDIENTS

FOR THE FILLING

2 pt (1 lb/500 g) raspberries

¼ cup (2 oz/60 g) sugar

FOR THE CREPES

4 eggs

1¾ cups (14 fl oz/430 ml) milk,
plus milk as needed

1 tablespoon light rum

⅓ cup (2 oz/60 g) all-purpose
(plain) flour

1 teaspoon sugar

½ teaspoon salt

1–2 tablespoons unsalted butter,
plus butter as needed

1 pt (500 ml) vanilla ice cream

8 fresh mint sprigs

STORAGE TIP: The crepes can be
allowed to cool and then stacked and
wrapped in aluminum foil and stored
in the refrigerator for up to 5 days.
Bring to room temperature or reheat
before filling and serving.

Strawberries, boysenberries, blackberries, or other fruits such as
sliced peaches or pears can be used in place of the raspberries.
For an extra-elegant presentation, drizzle the filled crepes with a
thin stream of melted chocolate.

SERVES 8

❋ To make the filling, place all but 8 of the berries in a bowl and sprinkle with the sugar. Turn to coat, then let stand for 15 minutes.

❋ To make the crepes, in a bowl, whisk together the eggs, 1¾ cups
(14 fl oz/430 ml) milk, and rum until blended. Gradually whisk in the
flour, sugar, and salt to form a thin, lump-free batter. If there are still
lumps, strain the batter through a sieve lined with several layers of cheese-
cloth (muslin). Cover and refrigerate for 2 hours. If the batter then
seems too thick—it should be the consistency of thick cream—thin
it by beating in a little milk.

❋ Place a 12-inch (30-cm) frying pan, preferably nonstick, over medium-
high heat. Flick a drop or two of water into the pan; if it sizzles and spat-
ters, the pan is ready. Drop in 1 teaspoon of the butter. When it melts, tip
the pan from side to side to coat the bottom. Pour a scant ¼ cup (2 fl oz/
60 ml) batter into the pan, quickly tipping and rotating the pan to coat
the bottom evenly. Pour off any excess batter. In a very short time, about
1 minute, the batter will begin to have bubbles on its surface, to dry at
the edges, and to pull away from the pan. Using a wide spatula, turn the
crepe and cook for only 30–40 seconds on the second side. Transfer to
a plate and keep warm. Repeat, adding more butter as needed, until all
the batter has been used. You should have about 16 crepes.

❋ To serve, place several spoonfuls of the berries in the middle of a
crepe and roll it up. Repeat until all the crepes are filled. Arrange 2 crepes
on each plate. Place a scoop of ice cream alongside each pair of crepes
and top the ice cream with a reserved berry and a mint sprig. Serve
at once.

NUTRITIONAL ANALYSIS PER SERVING: Calories 234 (Kilojoules 983); Protein 7 g;
Carbohydrates 28 g; Total Fat 10 g; Saturated Fat 5 g; Cholesterol 134 mg; Sodium 221 mg;
Dietary Fiber 3 g

Nectarine and Gorgonzola Bruschetta

PREP TIME: 20 MINUTES

COOKING TIME: 5 MINUTES,
    PLUS PREPARING FIRE

INGREDIENTS

3 nectarines

1 teaspoon lemon juice

12 baguette slices, cut on the diagonal

¼ lb (125 g) Gorgonzola cheese

COOKING TIP: For the creamiest, most spreadable Gorgonzola cheese, look for the type labeled *dolcelatte*, Italian for "sweet milk."

The classic dessert combination of fruit and cheese with bread is given a new presentation by grilling the bread and spreading it with Gorgonzola before topping it with chopped nectarines. Other complementary combinations include Brie with pears, Camembert with apples, and fresh goat cheese with dried apricots and pecans. Bruschetta is an especially good ending to an outdoor meal cooked on the grill. Toasts, cheese, and fruit may be served separately, allowing guests to assemble their own.

SERVES 4–6

❈ Peel and pit the nectarines. Finely chop and place in a bowl with the lemon juice. Toss gently to combine and set aside.

❈ Prepare a fire in a grill, or preheat a broiler (griller). Place the bread slices on the grill rack or on a broiler pan in the broiler about 3 inches (7.5 cm) from the heat source. Toast, turning as needed, until browned, about 5 minutes total.

❈ Spread each piece of toast with a generous teaspoon of cheese, then top with a layer of nectarine and serve immediately.

NUTRITIONAL ANALYSIS PER SERVING: Calories 306 (Kilojoules 1,285); Protein 12 g; Carbohydrates 45 g; Total Fat 10 g; Saturated Fat 5 g; Cholesterol 20 mg; Sodium 727 mg; Dietary Fiber 3 g

Strawberry Sabayon

PREP TIME: 20 MINUTES

COOKING TIME: 10 MINUTES

INGREDIENTS

¼ teaspoon unflavored gelatin

2 tablespoons warm water

3 eggs, separated

¼ cup (2 fl oz/60 ml) sweet Marsala wine

4 tablespoons (2 oz/60 g) sugar

1 pt (8 oz/250 g) strawberries, hulled and thinly sliced

Sabayon, a Marsala-flavored egg custard, is made light and airy by the last-minute addition of beaten egg whites. In this version, strawberries are folded in as well. Served in champagne flutes or other tall glasses, it is a refreshing finale to an outdoor meal in spring or summer.

SERVES 4

❂ In a small bowl, dissolve the gelatin in the water and set aside.

❂ In a nonaluminum bowl, whisk together the egg yolks, Marsala, and 3 tablespoons of the sugar. Place over (not touching) simmering water in a pan and cook, stirring constantly with a spoon, until a thick custard forms, 5–7 minutes. To test, dip the spoon into the custard and draw your finger across the back of the spoon; it should leave a path. Stir in the gelatin mixture. Remove the bowl from over the water, cover, and set aside to cool.

❂ Place all but ⅓ cup (1½ oz/45 g) of the strawberries in a bowl. Add the remaining 1 tablespoon sugar and mash with a fork to make a purée. Cover and refrigerate the reserved strawberries until needed.

❂ When the custard is cool, place the egg whites in a bowl and, using an electric mixer, beat until stiff peaks form. Using a rubber spatula, stir one-fourth of the egg whites into the custard to lighten it, then fold in the remaining egg whites just until no white streaks remain. Fold in the crushed strawberries. (At this point, the sabayon can be covered and refrigerated for at least 2 hours and served chilled; stir well before serving.)

❂ Spoon the sabayon into 4 glasses or bowls, garnish with the reserved strawberries, and serve.

NUTRITIONAL ANALYSIS PER SERVING: Calories 144 (Kilojoules 605); Protein 5 g; Carbohydrates 18 g; Total Fat 4 g; Saturated Fat 1 g; Cholesterol 159 mg; Sodium 50 mg; Dietary Fiber 1 g

Warm Ginger Cake with Peaches and Cream

PREP TIME: 35 MINUTES

COOKING TIME: 45 MINUTES

INGREDIENTS

¼ cup (2 oz/60 g) unsalted butter, melted and cooled

¼ cup (3 oz/90 g) dark honey

I egg, lightly beaten

¾ cup (6 fl oz/180 ml) milk

I tablespoon peeled and finely grated fresh ginger

I tablespoon ground cloves

½ teaspoon ground mace

I teaspoon grated orange zest

I tablespoon orange juice

1¾ cups (9 oz/280 g) all-purpose (plain) flour

1½ teaspoons baking soda (bicarbonate of soda)

FOR THE TOPPING

4 large, ripe peaches

I tablespoon lemon juice

2 cups (16 fl oz/500 ml) heavy (double) cream

½ cup (4 oz/125 g) sugar

ground cloves (optional)

This dense, spicy cake, lightly flavored with orange juice and zest, contrasts in texture and in taste with the sweet peaches and sugared whipped cream. It can be served with other soft fruits in place of the peaches, such as orange sections or sliced bananas.

SERVES 6–8

✳ Preheat an oven to 350°F (180°C). Butter a 9-inch (23-cm) square baking pan with 2-inch (5-cm) sides.

✳ In a large bowl, stir together the melted butter and honey, then beat in the egg. In another bowl, stir together the milk, ginger, cloves, mace, orange zest, and orange juice until well mixed. Pour the milk mixture into the egg mixture and beat well. Sift the flour and baking soda into the egg-milk mixture and stir until well blended. Pour into the prepared pan.

✳ Bake until a toothpick inserted into the center comes out clean, 30–40 minutes. Transfer to a rack and let cool in the pan for 10–15 minutes.

✳ While the cake is cooling, peel and pit the peaches, then cut into slices. Put the slices in a bowl, drizzle with the lemon juice, and turn to coat. In a bowl, using an electric mixer, beat the cream until soft peaks form. Slowly add the sugar, continuing to beat until stiff peaks form.

✳ To serve, cut the warm cake into squares and place on individual plates. Place a spoonful of peach slices alongside each piece of cake. Top the cake with the whipped cream and dust with ground cloves, if desired.

NUTRITIONAL ANALYSIS PER SERVING: Calories 549 (Kilojoules 2,306); Protein 7 g; Carbohydrates 56 g; Total Fat 34 g; Saturated Fat 21 g; Cholesterol 146 mg; Sodium 304 mg; Dietary Fiber 2 g

GLOSSARY

ARTICHOKES

Plentiful during spring and summer, these unopened thistle heads bring a taste of their native Mediterranean to outdoor tables. When small and young, measuring no more than 1–2 inches (2.5–5 cm) long, artichokes need only minimal trimming. The pointed leaves of larger, older specimens grow tough and, along with the fibrous interior "choke" that also develops as the vegetable matures, must be stripped away to reveal the tender inner base, or heart. Mature artichokes are sometimes also called globe artichokes, a term that describes their shape and distinguishes them from the unrelated tuberous vegetable known as the Jerusalem artichoke.

ARUGULA

Found wild in its native Mediterranean and in other temperate regions, this distinctive green has small, elongated, multiple-lobed leaves that are enjoyed for the slightly bitter, peppery flavor they contribute to salads and other warm-weather dishes. Cultivated arugula, which is generally more tender and milder in flavor than its wild counterpart, may be found in well-stocked food stores, greengrocers, and farmers' markets. Also known as rocket.

AVOCADOS

Native to Central America, these vegetable-fruits were carried to North America and Europe by Spanish explorers and are grown today around the world. As a result, avocados are available year-round. The best tasting and among the most widely cultivated of the hundreds of varieties that exist, however, is the Haas avocado, which comes into season in spring and summer, when its buttery-smooth, cool, green flesh is most welcome on outdoor tables. The Haas variety is easily distinguished by its pearlike shape and very pebbly, greenish black skin. Both characteristics contributed to the quaint name by which it was long known in English kitchens: alligator pear.

BALSAMIC VINEGAR

For centuries, balsamic vinegar has been produced in Modena, Italy, according to a complex formula that calls for grape juice to be reduced and then aged for many years in a succession of ever-smaller barrels made from different woods, each of which imparts its own dimension of flavor. The resulting product has a rich, almost syrupy intensity that makes it a wonderful addition to salad dressings, sauces, marinades, and all manner of other savory dishes, as well as to fruits, particularly strawberries. Growing popularity has triggered an increase in products that are called balsamic vinegar, but may not be authentic. Seek out bottles imported from Italy that are labeled *di Modena* (from Modena) and that preferably include the number of years the vinegar was aged.

BERRIES

At their plumpest and sweetest during months when sunny weather entices us into the open

EQUIPMENT

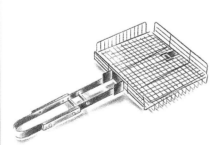

GRILL BASKET
Specifically designed to contain delicate items or small pieces of food, thus preventing them from falling through the cooking grid of an outdoor grill, this long-handled device consists of two closely spaced wire grids that securely clamp the food between them.

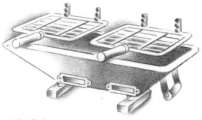

HIBACHI
Usually measuring no more than 1 foot by 2 feet (30 by 60 cm), this small, cast-iron or cast-aluminum grill allows convenient outdoor cooking in areas with limited space. Because of its size and lack of cover, it is best suited to quick, direct-heat grilling of no more than 3 servings at a time, requiring that recipes for 4 people or more be cooked in batches.

KETTLE GRILL
Available in a range of sizes, this fuel-efficient grill, suitable for direct-heat and indirect-heat cooking, is distinguished by its deep, hemispherical fire pan and domed cover, both of which are vented to allow ease of temperature control.

air, fresh berries are among the greatest pleasures of the outdoor table. Seek out each type in turn when it reaches its peak and is most plentiful: deep pink to red, heart-shaped **strawberries** thrive from early spring to early summer; spherical, smooth-skinned **blueberries** flourish from early June through midsummer; glossy, purple-black **blackberries** are available throughout the summer; juicy red, purple-black, or golden **raspberries** are also harvested throughout summer but are at their best at midseason; and harder-to-find **boysenberries** (below), large, deep purple hybrids of blackberries, red raspberries, and loganberries, appear in markets from early summer into the first days of autumn.

CHERRIES

A fleeting pleasure of early summer, cherries grow in temperate regions throughout the world. Several hundred distinct varieties have been identified, but most markets offer only two or three kinds. Look for dark red **Bings**, the most widely available type; rarer **Tartarians** and **Burlats**, which may be found in some farmers' markets; or such succulent varieties as **Royal Ann**, **Queen Anne**, or **Rainier**, distinguished by their red-blushed yellow skins and flesh. Sweet cherries may also be used in cooking. Sour cherries, including **Montmorency** and **Morello**, are used exclusively in cooked and baked dishes, their distinctive tang balanced by sugar that brings out their fruity flavor.

CILANTRO

Also known as fresh coriander and Chinese parsley, cilantro is a leafy herb whose seeds give us the spice known as coriander. The flat, frilly-edged leaves, which

CHILES

Many food stores now carry a wide range of chiles. For the best selection, shop at Latin American, Asian, or farmers' markets. Among the many varieties available, those used in this book include:

ANAHEIM

Large, slender green chile about 6 inches (15 cm) long and 2 inches (5 cm) wide. Mild to slightly hot. Also referred to as long green or California chile and similar to, but somewhat less spicy than, the New Mexican chile.

ANCHO

Dried form of the ripe, red poblano chile, distinguished by its brick red, wrinkled skin and its wide (*ancho* in Spanish) stem end, which measures about 3 inches (7.5 cm) across. Spicy but not excessively hot, it has a sweet, fruity edge.

ÁRBOL

Very hot, fresh or dried, red "tree" chile with slender, tapered body 2–3 inches (5–7.5 cm) long. Similar to the cayenne.

BIRD'S EYE

Variety of cherry pepper, similar in size, shape, and color to a cherry tomato and ranging from sweet to hot.

CAYENNE

Variety of very hot, slender red chile 2–5 inches (5–13 cm) long. The term *cayenne* also refers to a hot blend of powdered red chiles that may or may not contain true cayenne chiles.

HUNGARIAN WAX

Most likely so-named because it developed from peppers grown in eastern Europe, this fresh chile is also called a banana pepper because of its waxy yellow color and slender, slightly curving shape up to 5 inches (13 cm) in length. Both sweet and medium- to spicy-hot varieties exist.

JALAPEÑO

Familiar, fiery chile distinguished by its thick flesh and small, tapered body 2–3 inches (5–7.5 cm) long and up to 1½ inches (4 cm) wide at its stem end. Named after the capital of the Mexican state of Veracruz, jalapeños are usually sold green and less frequently red.

PASILLA

Dried chile notable for its rich, moderately hot flavor with a hint of sweetness. Slender and measuring up to 6 inches (15 cm) long, it has a skin as brown and wrinkled as that of a raisin, the fruit from which it takes its Spanish name. Known as a *chilaca* in its fresh form.

PEQUÍN

Tiny, slender dried red chile no more than ¾ inch (2 cm) long and intensely hot, with a sweet, smoky edge. Also called *chile pequeño,* or "small chile."

POBLANO

This dark green or ripened red chile resembles a tapered, triangular bell, measuring up to 5 inches (13 cm) long and 3 inches (7.5 cm) wide. Because of its widespread availability, generous size and shape, and mild spiciness, it is a popular candidate for stuffing.

SERRANO

Used fresh in its underripe green and its ripened red forms, this "mountain" chile is as hot as a jalapeño but with a distinctly sharper taste. Serranos generally measure no more than 2 inches (5 cm) long and ½ inch (12 mm) wide.

resemble those of flat-leaf (Italian) parsley, have a highly aromatic, sharp, astringent taste that especially complements the spicy dishes of India, Southeast Asia, and Mexico. Because cilantro wilts rapidly, it should be used within 2 or 3 days of purchase. To store fresh herbs such as cilantro, refrigerate them with their stem ends in a glass of water or wrap them in damp paper towels and slip into a plastic bag.

FAVA BEANS

Encased in long, green, flattened pods, fava beans are related to peas and, when fresh, share with them a wonderful sweetness and a tenderness that seem to capture the essence of springtime. Choose fresh-looking, plump green pods, splitting them along their seams with your thumbs to reveal the beans inside. The thin skin enclosing each bean is easily removed after the beans are briefly blanched. Also known as broad beans.

FIGS

Fresh figs, with their small, plump profiles and sweet, luscious flesh filled with edible small seeds, are one of the pleasures of summer. Among the varieties most commonly found in food stores and farmers' markets are green-skinned, red-fleshed **Adriatics**; small, yellowish green **Kadotas**, which have purple-pink flesh; and **Missions**, distinguished by their purple-black skin and intensely sweet, pink flesh.

GRAPE JUICE

The juice of unripe grapes gathered in early summer, also known as verjuice or by the French *verjus* (green juice), adds a distinctive, bright tang to savory warm-weather dishes. If fresh underripe grapes are unavailable, bottled verjuice may sometimes be found in specialty-food stores.

LEMON VERBENA

Spanish explorers discovered this highly aromatic shrub in Chile, and its use spread throughout Europe. The leaves, whether fresh or dried, impart a strongly herbal, lemony flavor to beverages and fruit desserts.

MELONS

Cool, succulent **cantaloupes** (below), named for the Italian town of Cantalupo, are among the most widely available of summer's melons,

abundant throughout the season and promising refreshment with every bite of their sweet, aromatic, and juicy orange flesh. The **Charentais** melon, related to the cantaloupe, is regarded as having an even finer, more highly perfumed flavor than its kin. Unlike cantaloupes, which have bumpy, tan, netlike rinds, Charentais melons have smooth-textured, creamy yellow-green skins with darker green stripes.

MOREL MUSHROOMS

Among the harbingers of spring and available through early summer, these wild mushrooms are prized for their cylindrical, dark brown, honeycombed caps, which have a rich, earthy flavor. Because of the caps' deep wrinkles and hollow centers, they must be thoroughly rinsed in several changes of cold water or, if especially dirty, soaked for several minutes. Trim off the stems before cooking. Look for morels in specialty-food stores or farmers' markets.

OLIVE OIL

The ripened fruit of the olive tree is pressed and filtered to produce an aromatic, flavorful oil that has long been favored in Mediterranean kitchens and is now enjoyed throughout the world. **Extra-virgin olive oil** is the highest grade of oil extracted on the first pressing without use of heat or chemicals. It has a distinctively fruity flavor and color that will vary depending upon the olive variety used. Extra-virgin olive oil is used primarily to contribute character to dressings or marinades or as a condiment. Products labeled "**pure olive oil**" have undergone further filtering and thus much of their character has been eliminated. Because they are less aromatic and flavorful and can be heated to high temperatures without burning, they are better suited to general cooking purposes.

OLIVES

Whether they are used as a featured ingredient, a garnish, or part of an antipasto platter, or on their own as an hors d'oeuvre, olives make a piquant addition to the casual outdoor table. Both underripe green olives and ripe black olives are cured using various combinations of salt, brines, oils, vinegars, and seasonings to yield a wide range of results. Well-stocked food stores and delicatessens generally carry good selections, sold either in bottles or loose by weight. Whereas some Mediterranean-style brine-cured black olives are packed in olive oil, brine-cured **Kalamata** olives from Greece come packed in vinegar. To pit an olive, carefully slit or halve the olive with a small, sharp knife and pop out the pit. Alternatively, use a special kitchen tool known as an olive pitter, which grips and holds an olive while a squeeze of its handle pushes the pit free.

PROSCIUTTO

The intense flavor and deep pink color of this Italian-style raw ham, a specialty of Parma, are the result of a time-consuming process. First pigs are fed a diet of whey left over from the production of Parmesan cheese. The hams are cured by dry-salting for 1 month, followed by air-drying in cool curing sheds for 6 months or longer. The unique qualities of prosciutto are best appreciated in tissue-thin slices. The ham may be eaten raw, on its own or to complement summer fruits such as figs or melon, or it may be chopped or cut into julienne strips to flavor cooked dishes.

SMOKED SALMON

Rose-hued salmon, one of the richest-textured, sweetest-flavored of fishes, takes well to smoking. It may be smoked by one of two methods: hot smoking, which also cooks the fish to yield flaky flesh, or cold smoking, which results in a silken texture. Unless otherwise specified, when a recipe calls for smoked salmon, purchase the cold-smoked variety, available freshly sliced in delicatessens and specialty-food stores and pre-sliced and vacuum-packed in the refrigerated cases of well-stocked markets. **Lox,** which is a salt-cured salmon, and **Nova,** another type of cold-smoked salmon, are also commonly found in Jewish delicatessens. They have oilier textures, however, which make them, in most cases, unacceptable substitutes.

SQUASHES, SUMMER

Small in size relative to their wintertime namesakes, summer squashes are characterized by their thin, edible skins, tender flesh, and mild flavor. The best-known variety is the cylindrical **zucchini,** also known as the courgette, which has dark green skin with creamy flecks and pale green flesh. Yellow-skinned and -fleshed **gold zucchini** may also be found; these resemble **crookneck squashes,** which in turn are distinguished by the swanlike curve

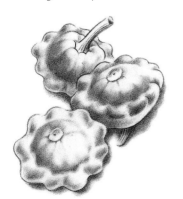

of their slender stem ends. Many markets carry the **pattypan squash** (below, left), sometimes called the custard squash, a pale green or mottled green-and-orange variety that resembles a slightly flattened spinning top with scalloped edges, and the similar but somewhat plumper, dark green **scallopini.** Among the rarer finds is the **Ronde de Nice,** a dark green squash that, as its name implies, is almost perfectly spherical. Smaller specimens of all types of summer squash will have finer flavor and fewer, smaller seeds.

TOMATILLOS

Once the loose, brown, papery husks of fresh tomatillos have been torn away, the small green fruits inside closely resemble green tomatoes, although they are in fact related to the Cape gooseberry. Like tomatoes, however, tomatillos are used exclusively as a vegetable, contributing their tart, astringent flavor to both fresh and cooked sauces, particularly in Mexican cooking. Most well-stocked food stores also carry husked and peeled tomatillos in cans.

WATERCRESS

Part of the mustard family, these crisp sprigs of round, dark green leaves contribute a refreshingly spicy flavor to salads and a distinctive garnish to other dishes. Watercress grows wild in freshwater streams in its native Europe and also thrives in commercial cultivation. It has the sweetest, least bitter flavor when picked during the cooler months of spring or autumn.

TOMATOES

Many tomato varieties, including a range of heirloom tomatoes, may be found in well-stocked food stores and greengrocers, and particularly in farmers' markets.

To peel a tomato, immerse in boiling water for about 20 seconds, then transfer to a bowl of ice water. The skins should then peel off easily, either with just your fingertips or with the assistance of a small, sharp knife.

To seed a tomato, cut it in half crosswise. Squeeze each half gently to force out the seed sacs.

BEEFSTEAK

Oversized, irregularly shaped, slightly flattened tomatoes with an intense flavor and meaty flesh.

CHERRY

Cherry-sized tomatoes, either red or yellow, with sweet, juicy flesh.

GREEN

The term commonly used for underripe tomatoes, which are prized for their tang and their crisp texture. Generally available at the beginning and end of the summer growing season.

PEAR-SHAPED

Small, juicy, and sweet bite-sized tomatoes, either red or yellow, and shaped like pears. Also sometimes called teardrop tomatoes.

YELLOW

Sweet, mild, and juicy tomatoes with bright golden skin and flesh.

INDEX

ACKNOWLEDGMENTS

The publishers would like to thank the following people and associations for their generous assistance and support in
producing this book: Desne Border, Ken DellaPenta, Jennifer Hanson, Hill Nutrition Associates, Lisa Lee, and Cecily Upton.

The following kindly lent props for photography: Fillamento, Williams-Sonoma, and Pottery Barn, San Francisco, CA. The photographer would like
to thank the following people for generously sharing their homes with us for our location settings: Eve and Terry Baldwin, The Mill Rose Inn, Half Moon
Bay, CA, and Mary Driscoll, San Francisco, CA. We would also like to thank Chromeworks and ProCamera, San Francisco, CA, and FUJI Film for
their generous support of this project. Special acknowledgment goes to Daniel Yearwood for the beautiful backgrounds and surface treatments.